T0113928

# THE DEVOTION, IN DEVOTIONAL POEMS

JAMES EDWARDS, JR.

WESTBOW
PRESS®
A DIVISION OF THOMAS NELSON
& ZONDERVAN

WestBow Press books may be ordered through booksellers or by contacting:

WestBow Press
A Division of Thomas Nelson & Zondervan
1663 Liberty Drive
Bloomington, IN 47403
www.westbowpress.com
844-714-3454

ISBN: 978-1-6642-4463-4 (sc)
ISBN: 978-1-6642-4462-7 (e)

Print information available on the last page.

WestBow Press rev. date: 10/20/2021

# CONTENTS

# THE ORDER OF MATURITY

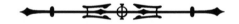

# THE BEGINNING[1]

It is my opinion that it would be appropriate to approach this idea with the understanding that it is the heavens and Earth with mankind which is being decided here.

No one can make it logical to put God in time and space, within the beginning of mankind.

So, in the beginning God decided to create the heavens and the earth.[2]

And, because darkness and emptiness were over the surface of the deep, God's Spirit was hovering over the waters.

If anything is to have a good intent, God's Spirit has to be involved.

There is a vast and even more huge complexity to the function of our heavens and Earth that is in the galaxy which makes up our universe.

To say that the universe just happened or evolved would probably require more faith than to believe that God is behind these amazing statistics of the universe's existence.

Nevertheless, I believe that God truly did create a wonderful universe.

So, in His infinite love for His creation of the heavens and the Earth, God spoke into existence everything we have to experience today.

Starting with light, the expansion between the waters, the sky, the dry ground called land.

God made the land produce living creatures according to its kind and the same with livestock and wild animals.[3]

God apparently made things and creatures we have never seen with such a large variety.

According to its kind, and He saw that it was good.

The land produced vegetation, seed-bearing plants and trees on the land that bear fruits with seed in it, according to its various kind.

God saw to it that we have a day and night, a morning and an evening.

He saw to it that we had a number of days and two large lights in the sky, one for day and one for night.

He also made the stars.

God said "Let the waters teem with living creatures,"[4] and He made the birds fly above the earth across the expanse of the sky.

And, with all His work He would evaluate His progress and saw that it was good.[5]

And, then with all creatures, as He did with mankind, God would bless them and said "Be fruitful and multiply on the Earth."

Here is what I understand: the expectation of God is that His creations would mature in their growth and pass down to others as they grow.

Establishing this moral concept would give you something of value to pass on to others, that includes your brothers, sisters, sons and daughters, siblings and the world.

Being fruitful is the value outlined in God's attributes and His word, which displays His character, His love, services, productiveness, honesty, integrity, and growing in faith.

God is our beginning; He is our present and our future.

# SALVATION

Salvation; it's my deliverance from me and the world of other men – relieved from a permanent stain of living in my own sin.

Time to discover my new place – in my new home, accepting the gift of being saved, and the fact that I'm never alone.

I am saved for life, a last breath with a price, paid in full for nothing I deserve – acceptance of a love with an open heart, not held back to reserve.

I believe we all need this salvation, a connection to the gospel and God's revelation.

We learn that Jesus' saving grace extends to the rich, to the poor, to the happy, to the sad.

No more living in the dark, I'm now reborn into a family that I never had.

It's an eye opener to learn more of the biblical side to this time and space.

How the world is moving at a high speed, "away from God" – and going no place.

It is my hope that the world would turn away from this Prince of Air.

If only we could, and would, share the vision of which God will make us more aware.

Salvation is the love that reconnects us to the Father, implanted in our hearts deep within;

Once the growth starts, then there's nothing that can separate us, not even the sin.

His love is stronger than death, it can't be killed by time and space, it's an essence created by God that can change anything! Including the look on your face.

You abide in the Lord as He in you, for God will lead you from the life of corruption.

Though wide is the gate and broad is the road that leads to destruction

God will make a change for you – "when you change" – since you can't change yourself; God will change you the way God changes, that way the change is really felt.

Truly, it's by God we know that the submission of others is for others.

It's part of God's plan that everything under His grace would be covered.

There's no condemnation, therefore ends with no separation.

This is a picture of our life in Christ.

Think confident; Christians are safe, Christ is around them, the Spirit is within them, and God is always for them.

It's to our benefit that we accept His plan for salvation; it starts in Genesis and then again in the book of Revelation.

God created the body that carries the soul that is guided by the Spirit.

And salvation is God's invitation, calling collect – from Spirit to heart; can't you hear it?

The Spirit gives life, and the flesh counts for nothing but a shell.

The world is too important to fall down and under Satan's spell.

If you don't know: Christ died for you.

And know that you died with Christ.

Now you are "free" to fellowship with Him, doing His will for the rest of your life.

We are saved by His grace and transformed by His love.

Are you not convinced?

Salvation is a need from the heavens above.

A transformation is being saved by His grace - and receiving salvation in and beyond time and space.

# DEATH TO MY FATHER

I stand before God the Father to say farewell to my Earthly Father, not goodbye; or why, just that I'll see you in heaven.

I'm confident like David, that God will not leave him in his grave.

I'm also confident, because of Jesus Christ, my Father was saved.

As believers we can be assured that God does not forget, when we die.

So, if you know God like I'm doing, you know He doesn't lie.

My father is in heaven with the Father, and left a legacy behind.

I think God would approve; He makes His whole family shine.

Death is necessary, it's part of God's plan, so we continue to pray and praise God, rejoicing while we can.

I am proud to be my father's son, likewise a child of God; giving praise to them both, to me doesn't seem odd.

God's provisions have a far greater purpose than helping us avoid pain; it's to make us better to serve Him just the same.

My mother has experienced my father's life; but only God knew his fate.

My siblings and I can agree: his life is worthy to emulate.

At the time of death, some may regret having less time invested without God while here on Earth.

I believe my father may have departed not knowing just how much family valued his worth.

As a maturing follower of Christ, he grew at forgiving, loving and caring.

As God embraced his life, these are qualities he didn't mind sharing.

"Therefore, we do not lost heart, though outwardly we are wasting away.

Yet inwardly we are being renewed, day by day." [6]

Like Jesus Christ; my father suffered awhile and then he was called.

So, we fix our eyes not on what is seen, but on what is unseen, to ensure our souls don't fall.[7]

So, death is at work in us, but life is at work in us too.

Knowing Jesus Christ: understand what this means and what God can do for you.

My father carried his cross for family to keep us moving forward; to sustain the soul, before the body is lowered.

Death means absent from the body[8]; I believe this is what God ordered.

From Jesus Christ, my father will be judged as a good man – measuring up to God's standard, he'll fit nicely into the master's plan.

My father has left the presence of this earth, though I'm not without a father because of my reborn birth.

So, life goes on; finding my place in my new family – I've adopted a different lifestyle with less of the world's calamity.

Still learning how to deal with the death to my father.

# MY LOVE I LOST IN
# A RAINBOW

The love of my life is my heavenly Savior.

The very one Who gives is also judging our behavior.

He has the right to examine and judge our character, our attitudes and heart.

While holding us all accountable for actions displayed – that would tear us apart.

It's the hope; is what Jesus has given to mankind, to choose a way of life that compared only to God's standard of time.

For those who know Him, also know He has an answer for everything.

We can cry out to God, for absolutely anything.

So, I did; I asked for a marriage that would line us up in the same row.

Aligning our lives with God, she became my true colors in a rainbow.

So now when I dream, I see orange, purple, yellow and green – I ask the Lord – take me by the hand – show me what it means.

Night after night I see another love of my life.

She just wants to be that part of me, who loves Jesus Christ.

She's my wife, I lost in a rainbow.

Our colors of marriage are what we have to show.

God is the glue that tied us together, that bond is a promise that will last forever.

To move forward after death – God told me, I can't do it alone.

There's a time to share, to love and grieve till God calls me home.

Life goes on; but even so, she will always be my rainbow.

The true colors of my heart are what I have to show.

I see red, purple, yellow and green – I see colors of life, only God knows what it means.

I hope it's her legacy that will always hold on to me.

Part of her is gone, but her spirit left behind for me to see.

It was a grand journey I lived with my wife.

Displayed the fascinating colors of life.

In my heart – I lost my wife in a rainbow; the longevity of our marriage is what I have to show.

I see orange, red, yellow and green, she was my rainbow of colors to be seen.

So, I lavish in the marriage that He gave – and cherish the memories that were saved.

Because I see the rainbow of colors that she made.

# OBITUARY

Only eleven days after her sixty-eighth birthday, Rebecca L. Edwards went home to be with our Lord. She was born Rebecca L. MacLoves in Honolulu, Hawaii on November 19, 1952 into a large family with five daughters and five sons. All of her life Rebecca was a strong caring person. I think she adopted the concept of putting others before herself even before God found her. She really loved family and friends, especially her son, Creighton MacLoves. She dearly loved her grandchildren, always wanting to be able to do more with them whenever she could. Becky grew to be a unique woman, always considerate of others. She was five foot, two inches, one hundred and thirty pounds of woman with joy, love and persuasion. At a young age she was very outgoing and loved to laugh. Her middle name should have been laughter, but the L in her name meant Leihua for flower. She was a flower to everyone who knew her. Growing up she was a handful, resulting in her ending up with her older sister Ulu. Together they moved around a lot and always maintained a close bond. She had three other sisters, Brenda, Anita and Sarah. The five of them were angels, anchored with the love and entertainment of their baby sister, Becky.

Becky adapted well to any environment. When she and James, her husband, became Christians she managed to fit right in everywhere she went. She always had her favorites, her favorite Pastor, her favorite sermon, her favorite color, her favorite songs and her favorite scripture, Psalm 139. No one but her husband James will ever know all about her favorites because God taught her to treat everyone as she wanted to be treated. God taught Becky that what is seen is temporary, but what is unseen is eternal. Becky was at peace with whatever God had in store for her. In her heart she held onto favorite scriptures in John 14, especially these words of Jesus: "My peace I leave with you; my peace I give you. I do not give to you as the world gives. Do not let your hearts be troubled neither be afraid.⁹" She was not afraid.

She leaves to mourn James, her husband of forty-two years, her son Creighton, her sisters and brothers and a host of relatives and friends who will love and miss her every day until they rejoice with her in heaven.

# BROKEN TABLETS;
# THOUGH UNBROKEN WORDS

God said: teach them my decrees, show them how I want them to live.

Some thousands of years later, still lessons to learn: How we take and how we give.

Moses had the faith that it took to care for thousands against incredible odds.

Though he broke the tablets, he understood the words that were given by God.

Also given were His terms, if we choose to accept, God's word is filled with provision and His holy precepts.

There were scrolls passed down to discern us in biblical terminology, intelligent dialect, basic instructions, the languages of love with eternal security.

But don't misunderstand, God still desires an honest pursuit in our own self-purity.

If we want to react with instincts consistent with God's will – we must develop habits of obedience, which prompts us when to be still.

I too remember the tablets that were broken – though God's word had already been spoken.

His power is His word and his words are power.

If we could pursue this concept, our strength grows stronger on the hour.

God spoke to so many; through the minds of man, in so many words.

To His commands – we listen, but just how many heard?

If by chance you've committed adultery, what have you broken?

And, if you haven't been honoring your parents, again what have you broken?

Do you feel a need to lie?

Know that God already knows, so there's no need to reply.

Would you have broken those tablets?

Though Moses did it out of anger and disgust.

Then know this: God will continue to do, for our sin what He must.

Those tablets were the work of God – writings that were the word of God – to speak what was right.

Opening the minds of those who seek to know God with a deeper insight.

For all the saints who care to know more about the Lord's will – clear your mind of preconceived thoughts, so God distinctively empowers you with skill.

The instruction manual that the Almighty has given is about God's expectations and the way we live.

In these words that I have spoken, is God's word that is never broken.

When we seek God to know His way – He gives to our hearts words to say.

Our God is always protecting and adding to our spirit – seeking His Spirit is how we are to be drawn near it.

With faith, I can see God's vision through my eyes – visions which are sometimes disguised.

Each of us has a place in God's service – while only God deserves the glory –I accept God with total belief about this story.

God has a fix for our brokenness, in case you never heard.

Broken tablets are not broken when we choose and say the right words.

The Ten Commandments were once broken tablets, but God has no broken words.

Broken tablets though unbroken words – understand His decrees – trust in what you heard.

God is always protecting us physically – and in spirit.

It's when we seek His holiness is how and when we're drawn near it.

I believe in the right to have unlimited goodness in my life, I don't want the Holy Spirit out of my life – and I wouldn't want Jesus to pass me by, that just wouldn't be right.

"Through faith" – I can see God's vision through my eyes – feel the touch of His grace - victory is on the rise.

I aim to learn more of these broken tablets and decrees He has given to us – I intend to get through it, I will get over it, not around it, but under it, nothing will stop me from doing it.

While each person has his place in God's service, but understand who deserves the glory.

"Like Moses" I accept my place with confidence of this story.

The ten commandments were once broken tablets, but "God" has no broken words.

# A BELIEVER'S WAR ROOM

There is but one book I read;

For me, in all my circumstances, I'm also amazed to find more books inside the book I read that addresses all other circumstances.

It's astonishing how some told and untold stories could give such a visible look – and all can be found inside this one huge book.

Nothing ordinary about this; its contents are divine.

Being of God, which makes it one of a kind.

Whether you believe or not, the truth of God can provide whatever you may lack – it's been said more than once, the Word of God is fact.

His Word is above any and all; it is the final authority – God's word addresses all issues, mastering all seniority.

God's Word can always be achieved through the power of the Holy Spirit; to be transformed requires your total submission, to be drawn near it.

If you understand, you have the insight to be a believer.

Committed to doing it God's way to be a successful achiever.

When it comes to applying God's word, maturity doesn't start with the oldest; the ingredients added to the usage of His word brings out the boldness.

To all believers; we face the challenges of the world, our strength comes from the belief in God's Word – let us vow to never go back to the way things were.

Because of sin, temptation and tribulations, they are the world's biggest fight – knowing what weapons to use is a better way to approach it right.

As individuals seem to have lost the power with God, its possible that due to the lack of fellowship – so strengthening the relationship would resolve that through the fellowship.

In your prayers, I would caution you to study the power of being the bride of an awesome groom – choose your battles with prayers; to fight in the believer's war room.

Taking prayers in secret to the God of this universe, while we practice being hospitable – God would expect us to rehearse.

Whatever you'd like to accomplish in life, I remind you; it's best done on your knees – I suggest talking to God in prayers, He's a better choice at fulfilling our needs.

We can imagine the relationship between Adam, in Genesis and the Creator.

Though spoiled by sin, God still shows us grace by giving us His favor.

Prayers give you peace of heart and mind[10] which draws us closer to God, one prayer at a time.

Let me remind you prayers should be rooted in God's word.

In secret, take it to the war room where its best heard.

I thank God we never have to rely on self – and without God, most will not remember how that felt.

To know what and how to pray, trust God, His Holy Spirit gives you what to say.

I sow this to you in hope that no one is doomed.

In secret, pray to the Father, for your brother, in the believer's war room.

# THE TITLES WE
# CHOOSE TO WEAR

**Summary**: There will come a time at some point of our lives when some will put a label on who you are. Whether just or unjust, we have to be responsible for living up to that label or not. Depending on your belief system will determine how you handle or acquire those characteristics that may lead to your spiritual identity and more... Why not learn how God wants us to wear these titles, or just to eliminate? No matter what or who you claim to be, God has a design and a way for us to wear those labels. If you're a follower of Christ; then put that on. If you claim to be a Christian, then wear it right. Any and all things of God are given freely with clear insight. My poem is written and called "The Titles We Choose to Wear."

It's painful to look back at our choices through the lens of regret, and feel the weight of our failures seeking redemption that hasn't happened yet.

Suffering for what one believes if often nothing to be ashamed

Short term pain is sometimes the only path to long term gain.

God opens doors for believers who have a heart for obedience, listen to His Spirit, have patience, then react with expedience.

They say what's to be if we listen to what they say we can't bear – if God says you can, its up to you: the titles you choose to wear.

There are girls who claim to be women, boys who've taken on man – and an element of confusion that the world just doesn't understand.

Nevertheless, when troubled – we ask for time, talent, treasure from each other – whenever, whatever you can spare.

If only we would be more serious about the titles we choose to wear.

When taking on different tasks and you run into those rules of complications, learn the resources that are reliable to build from God's word with application.

We can all be strengthened when viewed from the right perspective.

When given a direct focus, we use our resources with the best objective.

Though I am just a saint trying to fit into God's will – I can fail and still swallow God's standard to be fulfilled.

When the opposition is there, always in my face, to claim my title, I use the name of Jesus, things seem to fall in place.

We can thank God for those anointed mothers who can also be our best friend – suffering for our sake is what they do, though Jesus died for our sins.

So, what justifies wearing the title of a mother?

Could it be the fear of God and the love for others?

To absorb this title, should they have God's strength and endurance?

A real mother seeks God– which makes her a woman of influence.

So, when it comes to the rules of God's word to declare – because of the name Jesus – any title I choose to wear.

# MY WORDS; AS I READ GOD'S WORD

Lord, I thank you for your words; words that are a lamp to my existence[11], the words that stand me up to be strong, to fight off the resistance.

Your words that are laying down a path to my steps, for even my opposers to follow.

I trust your words to lead my soul to eat the right words to swallow.

Your words my Lord, are enabling me to truly comprehend; whatever my life is missing your words will defend.

Understanding your words gives me a clearer vision of my purpose.

Praying; for whatever is buried inside of me comes to the surface.

I pray that I will have a heart that is teachable and open to what you want me to know.

I desire your instructions to teach me how to feed my spirit as I grow.

Help me my Father, I need your diligence to fulfill my goal.

My life isn't worthy without as much of you poured into my soul.

Show me where I'm wasting time that could be better spent reading your word.

Speak to my heart, give me the ability to memorize what I've heard.

Lord, I don't want to be just a hearer of your word[12]; my faith says trust that your provision would be sufficient, whatever may occur.

I desire to be a doer who is transformed[13]; developing a behavior that looks like Christ.

Included is your spirit with such blessing that would change my life.

Show me when I am, and show me when I'm not – following your instructions is doing much without saying a lot.

God, it's your will for me to hear and follow with my heart, as a good servant, acknowledging all your creations as a work of art.

Praying that your words will correct me, revealing the true purpose of my attitude.

Reaching while in search for the right measure of maturity at the right attitude.

Believing your words will give me hope that I can rise above my limitations.

While serving you, I'm being strengthened to fight all the world's ungodly implications.

Thank you, Lord, for your words – as I read it, I'm thankful that I hear your voice speak and feed me.

I pray and meditate for your spirit to always be here to lead me.

Reading your words keeps me on that biblical path – so that your expectation of me is not cut in half.

My words will always be because of God's word.

And, as I read, God's word becomes clear to understand why God created the world, as I read the word of God.

# BECAUSE I AM A CHRISTIAN

**Summary**: Everyday some of us Christian's exercise our roles where God has placed us in carrying out different tasks that would help build on His Kingdom agenda. Some struggle as some serve; we pray as we learn which way God is leading us. Yet, some of us may be still standing where God found us. Not stepping up; when God says step. Not reaching out when God says serve. Not performing when God says help. God invited us to be in His family, and since we chose to be Christians, let's walk the walk that Christians talk. In some areas we should serve more, in some areas we can do more, in some areas we can give more, and in all areas we can love more. From Christian to Christian let's be all that God has called us to be; let's be inspiring as we inspire others to do as well, which brings me to this poem I wrote titled "Because I am a Christian."

When I say I am a Christian; I'm not claiming to be free of temptation.

Only my Lord and Savior is due an explanation.

It's because I am a Christian, I pray with confidence, believing God is on my side.

And, even when I get lost, Christ will always be my guide.

When I say I am a Christian; I should be trustworthy; knowing right from wrong.

Confessing that I am weak and need His strength to carry on.

It's because I am a Christian, I trust in the Lord to climb to success, and if I fail, I know He'll be there to clean up my mess.

When I say I am a Christian, I'm not claiming to be perfect, like everyone else I fall short, but God believes I'm worth it.

Because I am a Christian, I still feel the sting of pain.

So, when there are trials or tribulations, I just call on His name.

When I say I am a Christian, doesn't mean that I will have it my way all the time.

I do believe, when I'm present with the Lord; it's enough to ease my mind.

Because I am a Christian, I have the intellect to speak and not judge.

I also understand what Jesus meant by the drinking of His blood.

To focus and strive for what God has willed us to be, that child, that servant, that disciple for the whole world to see.

When I say I am a Christian, I'm not holier than thou, I'm just a sinner who received God's good grace somehow.

Because I am a Christian, I will live as if I were going to die tomorrow, learn as if I were going to live forever.

Proud to be a Christian.

And I say this because I am a Christian!

# THE WORDS: "LET THERE BE PASTORS"

Who do you imagine created the heavens and the earth?

And, from that dust of the land – who then formed man and thought to give him a mate, and call her woman?

The start of an institution called marriage.

Designed to grow and be above average.

In the history of God – from man, it looks as though He would fail.

But in the belief with wisdom, God will always prevail.

The same God that orchestrated disputes between Pharoah and Moses.

Our God of grace – showing mercy, even to those who oppose.

In another story the time came for God to test Abraham – given a task that would demonstrate Jesus as the lamb.

So, wonderfully crafted, God had a plan in this dramatic blessing, placed in the hands of leaders – to teach us all a lesson.

The words were said and that created pastors.

They intervene whenever, to every disaster.

For all who are in God's family, consider us all to be gifted.

Observe God's true pastors, inspiring us to be uplifted.

The words were said, then there were pastors, they are the anointed ones who by all means follow their Master.

And the words were said, they shouldn't be deprived of whatever they need.[14]

Addressing the saints who are committed and truly believe.

And the words were said: they shouldn't try to do it all; but instead, with the gifts within the church – the work should be equally spread.

And the words were said: hold them in the highest regard;[15] love with prayers, their prosperity will be enlarged.

Believe the help they give for us to become the church – preparing us all collectively to always keep God first.

Again, the words were said: I have made many to be wise.

Knowing God, this should come as no surprise.

And yes, God has a plan for every man.

So, God sent to us pastors to help us understand.

And the words were said: I've allowed the whole world to experience my grace[16] – for all saints know that my words are meant for only one race.

It's not only for the righteous, God has given us freedom of choice to this task – in your salvation, for the sake of others, we need to just ask.

To all God's people, we've been taught about storing earthly treasure[17] - since God addresses all issues – we will be held accountable for selfish pleasures.[18]

The Bible says bad company corrupts good character[19]- listen to pastors tell why; in God's word we'll live forever after.

It's not just pastors that should take up their cross – God expects His servants to serve so others don't remain lost.[20]

Why?

Because of God's Word.

# A PASTOR IS A PASTOR

To even mention a good man, do you know where to start?

Should we try by the standard God measures His own work of art?

If pastors are fed by God's Spirit their goodness we need not search.

Given divine instruction how to take care of God's church.

There are in the world followers and then there are leaders.

Good pastors step down from wherever to become God's achievers.

Pastors are appointed and some accept with little complaint.

Keep in mind, a pastor is a pastor but a saint.

Our pastors show no partiality with only God's restrictions.

They all are nurturing our spiritual growth by God's convictions.

They receive with thanks, things of the Father's creation.

Men who stand firmly on the word of God, the whole word and no abbreviations.

Being tested of self-discipline to have little to no restraint.

Just remember, a pastor is a pastor but a saint.

To be a church leader requires more of God than experience.

We witness their abilities; who but God gets them through their inexperience?

Being appointed to God's service, it empowers most with a passion.

Notice that some have learned to serve with their own godly fashion.

It's in the nature of God's love, our pastors have learned to pastor the multitude.

To be effective they must also say and sing with the godliest attitude.

Thank God!!

We are their inspiration as they inspire us too.

Their teachings fill our hearts to do better what God expects us to do.

We should believe it's to and for the gospel, our pastors are acquainted – just like we believe a pastor is a pastor but a saint.

Like all churches, we too have been given a mission – fulfilling our task, we can now see God's vision.

Our leaders teach of having the comfort from God's love, for you to see.

One Spirit compels our pastor to show and tell why God loves me.

Our church in its unity is how God keeps us growing

Passed down from God to our leaders, it's our gift in the knowing.

With encouraging words from our pastors, it's how we stay strong with God's desire.

From the weakest link, with love, we do not put out the Spirit's fire.

A seed was planted long ago in the minds of a few.

On the word of God, an idea of a church is what eventually grew.

We as a church, shouldn't be judged on the basis of quantity – but the way God would judge, measured by the substance of our quality.

We confess the gospel message has that universal scope – while God provides our church with that transforming hope.

God is the supplement that would truly nurture our soul.

Pastors are given a spirit that drives us towards our goal.

Once God anoints a pastor, his character is not as easy to taint, just remember, a pastor is a pastor but a saint.

Pastors are leaders who prep other leaders to lead God's people to salvation.

As eventually, we all are responsible for living out our own spiritual liberation.

Our church has been gifted with extraordinary leaders.

We plan to listen and listen to God's plan to become true believers.

In the church, particularly our church, Christians become disciples and disciples become saints.

Pastors become better pastors, while holding the title of a saint.

Most churches are fortunate to have one pastor showing how Satan's grasp is to be alleviated.

While we are a church with four pastors and us showing them how they are appreciated.

Our God is also our Creator, and Jesus is our Savior, and both are quaint.

We should be so blessed to have pastors – who is a pastor, but a saint.

# JESUS IS THE WAY

As I embrace the moment, waiting to exhale for the next –in my tribulations that are sometimes complex.

We look for the means to fulfill our dreams from one day to the next.

And there are times we work hard at hiding our pain; Jesus is the way that leaves us with the hope to bring on change.

But if you really; then believe afterwards, things will never be the same.

So, is it time to try something different?

Some have a need to feel more sufficient.

Let's see what happens when we pray.

To be convinced that Jesus is the way.

Not holding anything back – with sincerity, just call on His name – I promise it would be the end and the beginning of change.

When we exercise our right to make a choice – acceptance will position you to hear God's voice.

It was in the garden; way back when Adam lost his way – and in the book of Acts; Paul was blind until he found the Way[21].

Jesus said: "I am the way"[22] giving us a new kind of life today.

"No one comes to the Father except through me"[23] were the words spoken by He who set us free.

God's truth of what was, and what is to come; would be the message to all, not just for some.

We should thank God; that the Way has been manifest – it's because our Savior cannot be put to rest.

The incarnation of Jesus is the master stroke of love – and His Spirit lives in those destined to the heavens above.

The blood of Christ opened the way for a new covenant to be put in play.

Self-effort and personal gain won't get-cha there.

It's the love in Jesus – which is what He gives us to share.

In our hearts, with the Spirit of Jesus, we bring the fruit of lips.

And our words are what we confess, so we don't lose our grip.

In Jesus our sins are taken away – transforming souls now; and every day.

With God's word; we can rebuild the human race.

As we come boldly to His throne of grace.[24]

When the world cries out; some may be confused about how to pray: "Jesus is the Way."

So how do we hear what God has to say?

"Jesus is the way."

I like the sound of going to heaven someday.

"Jesus is the way."

When the world around us is falling, to our children, what do we say?

"Jesus is the way."

Even to live a better day, in a different way, we must learn to pray and believe!

"Jesus is the way."

# THE TRUE LIGHT

God created this world[25]; thus, the status is at a state of confusion – that is, without biblical engagement and spiritual infusion.

Every institution on this planet is infested with their own interpretation of truth; by man or God, whose values do you think are the most beneficial to you?

To a true believer, God has and will give you a sign – so, will you stand children of God and let your light shine?

Allow the Spirit of God to wash those thoughts of disregard.

Planting seeds of holiness to witness lives become enlarged.

It comes down to how well you carry your cross.[26]

God would like to know whose living in the light, unlike the lost.

Seeking God's favor – we need to become God's flavor.

Listen to the Holy Spirit telling you when it's time – children of God – live to let your light shine.

It was Jesus who said "I am the true light"[27] – it's through and for Jesus, we must fight the good fight.

Staying focused to God, we should understand what He most desires.

Avoid His wrath – casting down those eyes like flames of fire.

Stay self-controlled and keep the order – hear the voice of God like rushing water.

It is our time – "children of God," live to let your light shine.

Our Bible is the map to the kingdom throne – let's read it, study it, live it til God calls us home.

To let your light shine, we must know the true light – God gives us choices to share in our Savior's birthright.[28]

Believers are being fed with a spiritual taste, as Jesus connects eternity with time and space.

We must trust God and be willing to make amends – as He unveils more truth, with the confidence that we comprehend.

It is our time "children of God," live to let your light shine.

Our relationship with God should exceed with no limitation – according to scripture this is the Bible's implication.

Children of God this is our time – to live and let your light shine.

As we believe that Jesus is the true vine,[29] standing in sight as the true light.

It is our time, to live and let our light shine.

For those who believe, we follow Jesus to show us the sign.

Jesus is the true light, with a Spirit that stays bright.

# TO SERVE OR TO BE SERVED

I have experienced many things in this first part of my life.

I must say, the greatest influence has been the revelation of Jesus Christ.

I've learned about how and why Jesus came – for us on earth – it's all the same.

It's never been a real mystery – His birth, death and resurrection tell more of His history.

There is a human side to His existence – said many who witnessed His persistence.

He was or became many things as this story unfolds – He was later well known to the people for saving souls.

He was a builder who specialized in transforming minds[30] – unleashing His Spirit[31]; to be sure we align with God's design.

From the beginning, Jesus was on a mission to fulfill His Father's will.[32]

If you're seeking Jesus for salvation – the reward is eternity, as the Lord reveals.[33]

In His list of assignments, you may have heard, Jesus came to teach us life; and how to serve.[34]

This means giving up for the sake of others – while adopting a new tradition of praying for your brothers.[35]

We must practice to imitate our Savior – it means to intentionally commit, the way Jesus approves is to submit, as His Spirit spiritually permits.

Being transformed to a servant: we must listen to God's Word – change your life with others, submit to God and serve.

We can thank God Jesus invested in us – for our sins we were saved – time to invest in Jesus – give back a little of what He gave.

God created and designed man to be in His image;[36] to grow old in His spirit – being loved with vintage.

To truly serve our Lord, we must truly serve each other – there's a blessing in this action, as we serve to one another.

God compels us to abandon the attitude of "what's in it for me," and adopt a new attitude of "I believe, even though I can't see."[37]

Since the beginning of time – time itself has no reward; except when serving time, value only what you can afford.

With the right attitude, it's the serving attitude I'm trying to promote, so Christians can grow strong against Satan and not be provoked.

As being encouraged – and encouraging others to serve, is another way to give while you're being purged.

Our love for others should be of the same kind – this goes beyond affection, it's a renewing of the mind.

This practice at the same time, is falling into His grace, loving others while learning to serve – as we serve the human race.

Hopefully our action to serve will influence others to serve, and not just while enjoying the luxury of being served.

# MY FRIEND IN GOD

Close your eyes and "imagine" God is right by your side.

The Lord is my Shepherd - When in need He is my Guide.[38]

He makes me lie down in green pastures[39] – before I sin and even again after.

Always being a friend who restores my soul.

Giving me strength I can trust to reach my goal.

God shows me the path to righteousness for His name's sake[40] - even the blind led by Him would know which path to take.

At some point; we will walk through the valley of the shadow of death.[41]

But fear not! – God is there; He's on the right and He's on the left – With His rod and His staff, there to comfort me - my faith says God is present, whether I can, or cannot see

If God's without joy, or if God's with anger, "not with me" still, He would prepare a table in the presence of my enemy.[42]

My friend in God would anoint my head with oil[43] - with His fragrance in my life - nothing in me would ever spoil.

Surely goodness and mercy with love will follow me all the days of my life[44]

And because He loves the church, you and I have God given rights.

He's the friend we need when no one else will care.

To dwell in Him, within His house, means that He will always be there.

God can't be mad at us – "Listen:" when we live in God - He loves and lives in us – He's the God with love we can truly trust.

That's my friend in God.

# WHERE IS GOD?

A saint I am, so with God I do have a voice.

My goal is to please Him, and living godly is my choice

When we live right, God is a rewarder – you may not really know God so an introduction might be in order.

Who is God and where is He?

God is the master of all creation – setting the course for new life with no deviation.

The secret things belong to the Lord our God, though things revealed are not just to please us.[45]

God gives that and more, all in the name of Jesus.

As an expression of His love toward someone, He created people; His expression toward something, He created the world.[46]

Now He is trying to create something greater in us, something religions won't be able to hurl.

Whether you believe or not, God is real – it's through those who believe; God will make His appeal.

For those who accept Jesus will also have God's Spirit – those who oppose; my prayers for you to be drawn near it.

What God demands is that we worship and glorify only Him.

Believers: just take up your cross[47] – God will deal with the rest of them.[48]

Our God is everywhere since the beginning of all that exists – to be in God's presence relies on how you would persist.

Accepting Jesus opens doors that God is willing to give[49] – to glorify God is a reflection of how we are to live.

As we grow in God, He grows in us – deeply dwelling in Him and learning to emulate Jesus.

When we seek to know God, His presence is everywhere we are.

Keep up with your prayers that allow you to see beyond the stars.

Mysteriously the same God that created in Genesis left footprints in Revelation.

Being put on earth to receive our created purpose, which causes for celebration.

So here we stand with God: opening minds, giving provision, and helping the lost find their way.

As we accept God's Holy Spirit and grow, He teaches us how to pray.

Where was God when jobs were lost and then we got sick?

If we were given the choice between the Word of God and money; which would you pick?

No one has ever seen God, but the trinity; who stands together side-by-side

As God reveals His sovereignty - from God there's nowhere to hide.

And where was God when I needed a shoulder to cry on?

He "has compassion" – problems become overwhelming and I need direction – as spiritual growth becomes evident, we can trust God to be our protection.

Where God is, should be in you – His Spirit shows you how and what to do.

Once we all learn who God is, it becomes more accessible to say where God is, and where to start.

Because once we apply the who's and what there is to know, nothing can keep us apart.

God will always go and be where I go because knowing where God is, is knowing who God is.

# WHO GOD WOULD BLESS

We can hope to acquire good intentions, doesn't mean that we always will – making a request is sometimes just a matter of good people skills.

Ever had those days?

Need someone to listen to what's on your mind?

I believe God would; blessed are those who rejoice in God and delight in mankind.

To God, it matters how we care for each other – "have a blessed day," the least you should hope for your brother.

Don't be one of those who say "Hey neighbor, come back later."

A chance he would mistake you for some kind of hater.

God would do for you – so it matters that you do for others, that which God would want you to do.

God would bless those who look and seek only Him; that's to make His face shine on more than just them.

God would bless those with the trouble of facing rejection.

To show them with favor of His holy protection.

God would bless graciously those who've proven to be His child – versus mankind's grace, which is rare and lasts for just a little while.

God would intentionally turn His face towards those who seek His approval.

Within salvation means no one or nothing can cause your removal.[50]

As people of God, we are to reflect His image in our attitudes in action.

So, we can function today as a biblical fatal attraction.

Our God would bless those who would willingly provide for others in need.

When requests are made to God, understand the promises of God's Word we should read.

Be reminded to glory in God's kindness, we should wear His kindness – kind hearts are His gardens, and kind words with such colors; kind thoughts that grow deeper than roots, and kind deeds that are the flavoring fruits.

Our God would bless the members who share in the body of church.

It was suggested that we seek God with the time we have left on earth.

I believe God would respond to your confession, and God would forgive all your transgressions.[51]

Our God would bless those who choose to expose their sin.

The blessing would start the moment you submit to the Lord, then accept Him as a friend.

# YOU'RE EVERYTHING
## THAT I NEED

Have you ever really thought?

The one thing in your life that you just couldn't do without?

Would it be people?

Or something too private for you to talk about?

I often think: what it is that I value, or what matters to me?

To be real, does it have to be something that I can see?

Does my faith have a face?

Would my hope take up so much space?

When I pray, can I say that it just disappears before going up there?

Or, should I pray and believe that God truly cares?

I've opened a relationship and established my walk.

It becomes visible as my actions reflect the love that I talk.

In the Bible, Paul had a way of expressing his love for his brothers – it became important for him to imitate Jesus with an attitude to serve others.

God is always watching for a willing heart to help drop a seed.

With God's blessing I'm bold to confess: He's everything that I'll ever need.

To be a servant of the Lord is what matters to me – it's God who gives me strength to be the best that I can be.

Sometimes we're led to other sources outside of God; somehow still under His guidance.

Committed to the same cause, forever dedicated to our alliance.

We should work with what we know, but always want to know more.

Never knowing enough, but in pursuit of Jesus – we're better off than before.

In order to reach more people, we should have a heart to teach more people.

After being saved the Holy Spirit will show you how to seek more people.[52]

It's through Jesus who sustains me – it is God's Word that empowers me – and it is my fellowship with God that assures me of the love that He has for me.

God is my everything that I'll ever need.

And I would still like you to pray for me.

This is the fellowship that will keep God pleased.

Slowly as we seek more of God, a transformation should take place[53] – God expects His will to become yours, as He shows us His grace.

I have a thirst for God's Word because I need to survive – as we praise and glorify God; He in His mercy will provide.

Claiming to be a saint with every breath that I take, all that has happened is by design, even the mistakes that I make.

As you seek your true worth – while others seek out of greed, remember the Creator: you eventually agree, God is everything you'll ever need.

The desire to feed your thirst – will be quenched by putting God first.

To know God, we need to accept His Son – the time will come when you and His Spirit are one.

I implore you to keep growing in faith with every good deed – and accept that God is everything that you'll ever need.

# PURPOSE

The name of my identity may not be as important as the reason for my serenity.

For I do have purpose.

I'm driven with a passion everyday – to perform and be used by God in some kinda way.

For I do have purpose.

To pursue such qualities as righteousness, holiness and soteriology – with the Holy Spirit's guidance, that would lead to a deeper theology.

I'm a simple man with simple needs, I pray like you, for the Lord to hear my pleads, for I do have purpose.

The Bible talks about Christians and others being at war – the world would trivialize the tribulation which we have opened the door.

In today's society; headlines may read of cheating, murders, adultery and rape.

The righteous would flip the pages of the Bible to impact their fate.

For I do have purpose.

Everyday people are faced with wrong and right decisions, as the world gets more complicated, living without the Bible's divisions.

Some may never grasp the concept of Jesus taking His last breath.

So, the world needs to understand God's reason for Jesus being put to death.

Salvation is a gift, so to appreciate, God's Word must come first!

He gave us all purpose, a plan for the entire universe.

And so, I do have purpose; we all have purpose with the gift some may be one of a kind.

It's for the others that God rewards with the spiritual renewing of the mind.

So, be encouraged, for in our purpose we get to know God in every season.

As in the Bible, Matthew, Mark, Luke, and John give us all the right reasons.

My purpose is what Jesus intended for all of mankind.

To love and care for all of God's creations at the same time.[54]

For we do have purpose; what will it take for us all to do a self-evaluation?

An assignment for us all; before Jesus returns to judge the world's population.

It becomes justified to ask: do you have purpose?

Then listen for God to say: I'll raise you up for the very purpose of revealing to you a measure of my power.

If not now, in and beyond every minute of every hour.

For "I" do have a purpose!

# I AM MY FATHER'S HAND

One day I awaken: I felt lost without a plan; I examine my heart, and in my mind, I realized my life was in my Father's hand.

I remembered when reading the Bible – I am to be my brother's keeper, expected to be Christlike – with God it runs much deeper.

I'm allowing the Holy Spirit to do its work inside of me – I wonder: when others look in my direction, just what might they see?

Good or not so good, with God would be a plan – He's in control and my life is in His hand.

If I do nothing, I could become useless, though my days are productive, sometimes I feel fruitless.

To be strong, I must move on and listen to God's command – being of service to others, that I too may be my Father's hand.

When we look in the mirror – do I dare ask?

Just what do you see?

I have a vision of a saint and my God looking back at me.

Like Moses was to God, I will take my stand – serving Him and others, that I may be my Father's hand.

God with His own Spirit flavors us to be the salt of the land.

So, to my Lord I receive and give praise as I lift up holy hands.

Though I'm still learning; with God one can be a difference.

Paul was the hand that showed us, His grace is sufficient.[55]

As God teaches to care for others – lend a hand – take time for a brother.

Even from afar we should hear each other's plea; God's favor comes as we rescue others in need.

Working hands together; God will protect us and hand over to us, the forces that come against us.

He always has a plan – and until I'm called home, I will be my Father's hand.

Because I care, I will make myself available, being a Christian I am not incapable – because I have faith; I'm free to believe – I'm living in His will, in this world to achieve.

Because I've inherited this image of the Father, I know I am love – focused only in the treasures found in the heavens above.

It is in my nature to be reflex driven, but also upright to share the gifts God has given.

I must confess: God has made me a humble man; because of that I have the heart to be my Father's hand.

As God's Word teaches, our lives will expand – so that we complete together God's purpose with each other's hand.

We've all been given choices to do the best we can – and adding God is more rewarding to every woman and man.

So, make that intentional act of answering others in need – with love; so that, to our Father He would be so pleased.

The Christian's purpose is to fit our lives into our Father's plan and as we learn we can all be our Father's hand.

# I'M GROWING IN MY FAITH

I imagine we all were born and not understand who we really are; given a name is the one thing that sets us apart.

Even though we're exposed to different truths, we were all created from the same roots.

Our journeys in life are branched in many different ways.

With only one God: we become God's people who pray.

I truly believe in the One we need to honor; His Spirit teaches how to wear His armor.

To our God, with Him, we wanna be upright – because with Him much pleasing to His delight.

Walking with confidence, you and God in relation.

Building faith involves choices; our lesson involves dedication.

Whether the spirit of a saint, or a sinner, we all have a choice – to build having more faith; with less, or to move with little faith, not to be deprived of the best.

When we speak of faith, about your faith: include the action that expresses the faith – because the day may come when it impacts your fate.

Acknowledging your belief, and the confidence given by the Lord.

He's nurturing all saints to draw them closer to one accord.

For the world, there are expectations that include a declaration, for the sake of your salvation.

Our God wants us to grow in faith – not to procrastinate, which could be your biggest mistake.

I would dare to question whether God's love or faith are real.

I believe it's designed to offer a flawed system a more valuable deal.

Where's the hope that God gives?

It's where your faith would start.

Your belief is the formula that eventually reshapes the heart.

There are some who may not be righteous, yet living in God's family.

My heart is still troubled by the multitude trapped in the world's calamity.

I know my faith will grow as prayers get around.

The gospel should be heard so that starving souls can be found.

I thank God for the world's sake, I'm still growing in my faith.

Sure, there are some who may be closer to God than others – what's good for me may not be as good for my brothers.

I do realize that I need God in every area of my life.

Faith is necessary to comprehensively move me closer to Jesus Christ.

It comes down to the choices that we make – how valuable; as much faith will it take?

Without God in my life, I cannot; I also know without me, God will not.

So, I'm still growing in my faith.

# I'M LIVING ON THE STREET OF FAITH

One day it was time to move from the home built with the hands of my parents' skill.

I'm in search for a spiritual foundation that would fit me into my Father's will.

Life is its journey; moving from place to place – lost as we are, some may obtain stability; only by God's common grace.

As I move to a dominion which I thought to be success – I've learned through others, time after time, I was building a mess.

Then, while reading the Bible, I came across a book called John, which gave me direction.

I must say, I was in awe, then I realized his words had spiritual connection.

And, there were others, such as Moses, Isaiah, Joshua, Joseph and Jeremiah.

So, I've invested in this property called theology; to see how it applies to the life of reality.

I've learned to just follow Jesus in your heart is not enough, you must show your faith by changed behavior, even when life gets rough.

Still, my goal is to live on this street called Faith.

Working overtime to learn something God calls His grace.

I've learned that God has given to us all that is needed for us by our Savior called Jesus.[56]

Also given to us are the tools to fulfill our goals, which for some of us would eliminate those waves of strongholds.

Growing into salvation; giving roots to our eternal security, trusting the Holy Spirit to produce my self-purity.

The beginning to no end, is just the first layer – next would be to establish a relationship in our Lord's prayer.

I'm one step closer to living on this street of Faith.

Our Father has fashioned this world to His likeness – no other theory can compare.

If only we would search our own hearts – we'd notice His fingerprints everywhere.

Only some know, that Satan is cunningly clever,[57] deceiving us all, occasionally attacking the strong – causing them to fall.

I've been told to build on faith we must believe with no doubt.

First open your hearts, for God will show you what seeing is about.

I've learned to reach that platform of faith is not about having the ability – but as you grow into a child of God, you will accept the responsibility.

I'm one step closer to living on the street of Faith.

Sometimes in life, we entertain temptation, causing us to detour down those roads of doubt.

Jesus is the map that would lead you, then show you how to turn about.

Faith as I know: I now know faith is being sure of what we hope for and certain of what we do not see.[58]

Could it be?

From a different perspective I see that God is living in me.

Or, could it be the visible demonstration of the comprehensive rule of God over every area of life?

Now I know, to know Jesus - it's possible to be born, not once, but twice.[59]

I'm one step closer to living on the street of faith.

Because I know God: God I now know because I talk to Him, because I read about Him, because I worship Him, because I minister about Him.

I know my God because my God lives in me.

I'm now living on the street of Faith!!

God can choose you, like God chose me, just for the world to see that He's living in me.

# IN THE IMAGE OF GOD

In the beginning there was only God: Being the only God, He is the world's only head.

After making the birds and other creatures, being fruitful is what God said.[60]

And then He said: Let's make man in our image; He can rule over the fish and sea.[61]

God had a plan for His land, and it included you and me.

First there was man and then He made woman for man.[62]

The expectation is for both to be redeemed, fitting into His master plan.

What God made, He expected to be in His image and watch us grow – He would issue assignments, to see maturity and give us prosperity according to the seeds we sow.

Seeking His approval: there are many ways to be judged by the Father – think of us as the wet clay, and He as the master potter.[63]

Having a covenantal relationship with God should be our intentional mission.

As servants to the Lord, being obedient puts us in the best position.

Although God reveals Himself through nature and the Bible.

Through faith we can trust God's Word to be reliable.

God is intentionally gentle with all you would ask Him to do.

So, in what or whose image could anyone compare our living God to?

To be blessed by God is in being a blessing to someone else to receive – for the redemption of our souls, we can expect God to retrieve.

Being in the image of God requires us to have more of His attributes.

Even such characteristics can be acquired with an adjustment of your own attitude.

Constantly we're in need to be fed with God's Word, which is an impact on your faith, influenced by what you've heard.

Being in the image of God as an individual, is an expression of my identity – being in the image of God as the body, identifies me in unity – and together as the church, worshipping God, loving people and using things to do God's work.

New creatures we are; heaven bound thus far – walking in the image of the invisible God, serving the firstborn of God's creation, leading us to eternity into our new destination.

We were all made in His image, but the only way to look like… we must train ourselves to think like … by the power of the indwelling Spirit – we will be like …God.

Whatever may influence a bad attitude, is still a bad choice.

By God's grace, through prayers we may have a more influential voice.

God's attributes are the image that believers need to reflect – in hopes of drawing others to receive and respect.

Christians are children of God learning to walk in His image – living in the light of God makes us the best of His vintage.

It's time for my prayers; if you are, continue to walk in God's image.

I'll be praying for you – because God is watching you too.

# GIFTS AND THE GIFTED

It is such a blessing to have been given a gift, thus every man has his own gifts from God.

Some are aware, others claim but never declare.

God's purpose, is that the gift that is given be used for His glory – along the way encouraging others with a testimonial story.

It doesn't matter if you're wealthy or don't have as much as he – consider God's gift the blessing of your eyes because they can see.[64]

In your heart, see the gap between God and His people tore down – with a gift from the Spirit, by word of mouth, believers have been found.

God personally invites us to be citizens of His eternal kingdom.

He appoints gifted people to collect songs and then sing them.

It is a gift for you to use well whatever you have.

Honoring God with gratitude for the sacrifice made on your behalf.

Gifts are presents that the receiver receives, but at no cost – God's love is reserving a place in your heart just for the lost.

With God waging war against the opposition it's already won – in spite of any odds.

A gift of great value to you is the best of you offered to God.

It's up to you to fulfill your created purpose as a servant to the Lord.

Gaining crowns is a way to nurture your growth, to serve God is your reward.

The Holy Spirit is a gift from our Creator of this world.

His love is given to all men, women, boys and girls.

To God, a gift of any kind opens the way for the giver, allowing easy access for our prayers to be delivered.

At the renewal of all things, through all we give for Jesus' sake, eternity is a life to be desired and God is waiting at the gate.

Living water is given to those who are thirsty for God and His Word.[65]

And only Jesus can give this gift for our desires to be heard.

I consider it a gift, that our Father's promises have been kept.

Ascending Jesus into heaven, into the hearts of many – guiding our every step.

For all those who deliver God's words with such elegance – are the gifted.

Saints are being used with a purpose driven assignment that inspires souls to be lifted.

I pray that the one who lives in you will be seen as greater – for we live to serve A God with many gifts, known as our Creator.

I hate to – without God – face the days of calamity that are now here.

With the Spirit of Jesus that lives in me, hope can be seen – it's bright and clear.

If only we would apply Jesus' words with guidance and direction – our way of life would give us confidence with divine protection.

I must admit, I've been dreaming of a gift I'd like to give my God someday, that every man and woman would have on their hearts to pray – to let me God, share my supper with you.

There's a plate filled with love from me, and prayers too.

A cup that is surely full of faith, and a bowl of tolerance with no room for hate.

I'd add a spoonful of patience and some sprinkles of nice, toasted with respect to spread more God on my life.

Finally, offer a napkin that's made of joy, to wipe a smile on your face.

With a meal such as this, the devil would have no place.

The time would soon come for a new earth to start.

With a song of praise that should be poured out from our hearts.

With every gift given, if you could just see yourself, but see me too.

If we could just see us all in a world that's brand new.

Everyday of the week I see the Bible unfold, but see also Jesus – a gift for the human soul.

# ALWAYS WEARING YOUR BEST

Take a moment and look at yourself; do others have a clear view?

When you walk or talk does the world see the God in you?

To be known of God as God knows you – we should always wear our best.

"Think attitude" - why should God settle for anything less?

To know that I'm wearing it right, I look to God; He'll give me a sign.

The Bible tells me – we should be made new in the attitudes of our mind.[66]

So, on Sundays I begin with the hearing of God's Word.

After such worship I'm wearing the sermon that I just heard.

So, by Monday I'm wearing His magnificent grace – I check my attitude, I know He's watching – if I could just see His face.

So, I'm praying, and Tuesday finally gets here – I can feel God's Spirit, which gives me confidence; I have nothing to fear.

For the Word of God is living and active[67] – remember to pray, while still being proactive.

When the next day comes my character is in check – I'm wearing my best attitude with a Jesus intellect.

God's word is more than simply a collection of words.

Identifying with Christ can be inspiring and righteously superb.

Understanding God's precepts can be a challenging test – which is why we should practice our dress, while always wearing our best.

So, today is Thursday and I'm still not weary, but prayerful.

I choose not to worry because I'm learning to be more faithful.

Some Fridays are better than others, but here we are.

Still wearing my best – God's Word has gotten me this far.

Once more God will put this week to rest – whether I succeed or not, the goal was to always wear my best.

Here we are at Sunday again, looking to achieve nothing less, my attitude is better because I'm always wearing my best!

# WILL I EVER BE READY?

When I bow down in the presence of my heavenly Father, I'm compelled to think back and wonder, just why did he bother?

Like many, I was once broken, lost in disbelief.

Something of God came over me.

I'm rejoicing with God in His word that has set me free[68].

I've learned there isn't enough to know about God the Creator.

As we journey this life – know between Satan and earth, Jesus is the perfect mediator.

When searching for answers, I would seek God; He's the most reliable that seems to care.

The world is so big and busy, only with God's Spirit is my best way to prepare.

I ask myself; will I ever be ready?

To be more obedient, trustworthy and devoted to God's cause.

God would not, so I won't be held back because of my character flaws.

There are in the life of many, barriers which separate us from the family's love.

The Holy Spirit will remind you what's important - to always be connected to the Father above.

To endure life's tribulations that are put in my path – I trust God and sin-not; to keep me from His wrath.

Will I ever be ready?

To just listen to God, as the world around me crumbles, believing in God as he opposes the proud while giving to the humble.[69]

Can I ever be ready?

I know His existence means that I was always loved – "Jesus died for me," giving to all the gift of His blood.

Will I ever be ready?

To pass all tests that God Himself would employ, I learn to count my blessings that may multiply my joy.

I choose not to be labeled as some kind of pretender; with salvation at stake, to my Father in heaven I must surrender.

It's His love that will conquer the oneness that we must pursue.

Only God knows that hour Jesus returns for us all to be rescued.

Will I ever be ready?

My question is: will you?

# CAN YOU IMAGINE?

Who but God, should receive all; and what glory?

Who gave me the insight to even write this story?

To have a vision through scripture of living a holy life.

Being forgiven of my sins that someone else paid the price.

Our Father in heaven paints a picture He'd like to tell and show.

Imagine this life, if you can, how the Bible will help you to grow.

Can you imagine?

Living in a world where there will be no more pain – a new world created with a love that won't feel the same.

Can you imagine?

Worshipping our God is all we're expected to pay – receiving His love is a way to live from day to day.

So, can you or should you, measure your ways set by the standard from God above?

God wants people, though free to hate, choose instead to love.

It's the love where we learn how to die in self, and be prepared to lay down our lives for someone else.

I can imagine, being in a world where I'm accepted just the way God has planned, learning to remain faithful as I live out a life in God's hand.

Don't be afraid to step out of your feeling that you're weary to lose – the Bible gives you a vision of choice if it's God you choose.

Let God's words fill your memory, rule your heart and guide your life.

Imagine where the world would be if it had not been for one man's sacrifice.

One day we'll all stand in His presence to be judged and justified.

Understand now why God not only wants, but should be glorified.

I can only imagine living in His family with the best security.

To live with God's words that's leading to my self-purity.

Protected with the promises He made to our fathers; God shields us from unseen forces, because He's our heavenly Father.

So, if you're here when tomorrow comes, rejoice in what it brings – honor first born of God and ruler of all kings.

Can you imagine?

With a heart bigger than size, imagine all that with your mind and not with your eyes.

I can; can you imagine?

# GOD IS THE PERFECT INGREDIENT

Have you ever felt empty?

As though something was missing.

Or had something to say – just needed someone to listen?

Now, you know right from wrong, but you did it anyway.

Knowing you should be patient, but you gotta have it today.

Life has its consequences when we show lack of obedience.

To improve the character of self, God is the perfect ingredient.

The Bible says man should not live by the world's standards alone.

God's strategy is similar to talking with Him on the phone.

We can witness a change when the act of obedience is complete, preferably through prayers, God will know that it is He you seek.

When talking to God, often words can be used to stimulate – God would remind us that it is Jesus He wants us to emulate.

To elevate from one level to the next, God's life changing design becomes expedient.

Through faith, it's to our advantage to believe that God is the perfect ingredient.

Christ, while suffering, was made perfect, but then He always was; are you willing to flavor your life with the same cause?

We have the freedom to breathe God's air that we don't see.

Believe that God has also given us the choice to be born free.

It's not hopeless; when the world considers the things you've held in your hands.

Have you held the best from the best, receiving the best from God's plan?

Choosing to be driven by the world; you will always have something missing – God chose His Son to be born, given the choice to die, so He had to be risen.

When the subject is God – likely there will be disagreement; no doubt in my mind – God remains to being the perfect ingredient.

There are some who have many choices and there are others who have little to none – living the way God chooses – we're entitled to an inheritance with the second coming of His Son.

So often we struggle with little; trying to gain more of what we had in the past.

The choices we make will determine the outcome when choosing God first or last.

For the prosperity you seek will dictate the goals you reach, with His essence – we'll find in His words, for the child of God to teach.

Accepting all God's ways, with no grievance, is the acceptance that God is the perfect ingredient.

God is the perfect ingredient!

# A PRAYER FOR MY BROTHER

My God, here I will stand – and I'm reaching for Your hand.

It was you who decreed – no longer am I lost.

I'm so thankful you chose Jesus to pay the cost.

I now have the choice to build a foundation – that would suit my life and impact my salvation.

To accept our Savior was a choice like no other – now I'm compelled to always pray for my brother.

It is my hope that every saint who follows our Christ – be assured of this security which Jesus paid the price.

I can think of no other act of obedience, that would change and cleanse our lives through the experience.

Because I chose salvation – I'm saved; I'm convinced of eternal security – I'm secured; and I have been baptized, touched by the Holy Spirit; before I realized God said do for one another.

So, I'm compelled to pray for my brother.

I have an advocate,[70]we just ask to get near it – I get closer to righteousness through the power of His Holy Spirit.

Having a desire to walk with Jesus, while holding the hand of your brother – to live under God's covenant, fearing no harm from others.

We as believers are free to live as God created us to live.

Praying for your brother is just another way to give.

Let's not pretend to be happy when faced with tribulation – instead call on the name of Jesus and change the situation.

Those with Jesus can be broken in their walks, but with faith, not bent in their thoughts.

Discipline your hearts to reach out for your brother.

And, allow your reach to extend much further.

As I pray, it is my hope that God's angels will have something to rejoice,[71] and because of our efforts, souls will be saved when we make the right choice.

But if by chance the world sees and says there is no God, we can't be strong; erase their doubts, because our God is ready to prove them wrong.

What do you have to worship?

With the proof that's greater – than Jesus and Spirit of our God the Creator.

It's because God's word is so reliable – our influence should come from the Holy Bible.

When it comes to God's truth, be careful who you don't tell – it's important that we don't just watch the world fall under Satan's spell.

I think God would want us to encourage each other – and clothe yourself with humility towards one another.

Look in the mirror – because one day you may be the one that needs prayers from your brother.

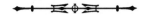

# GOD'S GRACE

We all know that God is always good; because I believe, wouldn't say different if I could.

He makes so much possible: He's too good to be true.

Miraculously He inserts His Spirit everywhere, for the believers to view.

There are too many features that make God so attractive – understanding the image of God requires you to be proactive.

To be better prepared we should seek to know our eternal place – having what you can't earn, that He gives is called God's grace.

Although the world has already absorbed much of His kindness, still out there are people in doubt, instead they choose to be mindless.

Believe it or not, God has set the course for mankind – we're at war with Satan, but if you believe, God can change your mind.

Because man - by God's standard is unique, our belief in God is what makes us complete.

Positioning ourselves to be in the right place when it's time.

God will reveal Himself as the only One of His kind.

In the most unexpected times, people will need a helping hand.

If our total focus is God – then our trust is on Him, not in man.

God has a genuine purpose of putting the right people in our life – two steps forward and one back becomes about getting to know Jesus Christ.

God grants us access through faith, His grace; it's when we believe, then trust, an exchange takes place.

God is perfect; and nothing in His character can be erased.

I praise God for being faithful; and extension of His grace.

God makes available for all saints at least one angel He assigns;[72] to be influenced more of Satan than God – hinders that design.

It's to our favor – the evidence in our deeds, we see God's face.

Always something of good measure that comes with His grace.

There are ingredients in the grace added with divine love and protection.

An adequate amount of compassion, with an adequate amount of affection.

God has already given the world much of His grace.

Receiving access to even more depends on your true face.

It's important to not measure in your giving, for God has his own biblical folder – that is: good measure, pressed down, shaken together and running over.[73]

If truth be told, we all have been spared by His grace; commonly speaking it is to our advantage to seek His divine love to be embraced.

With the hope of receiving all of God's grace.

# TRUE PEACE IS WHEREVER YOU ARE

Let's pause; and focus on our God and His much-anticipated wisdom; to maybe find favor to something that would reveal to us His system.

Are you not convinced?

That no eye has seen, nor ear has heard – no mind has conceived what God can purge.[74]

Is it right for me to lift up my hands showing gratitude for being included in God's plan?

Love is the message that God would like to give to us all – we can have and hold His peace, as we wait on His call.

Do we cry out to a God who already knows our heart?

As we do for the sake of others, we're rewarded a brand new start.

I believe it's true, my life is not my own – to pretend; God will reveal to show, just how much we're wrong.

When seeking God, I dare not hold back any praise, as God who prepares, He gives to us, all the reasons to declare.

To all believers, always be encouraged and let's be for real – seeking God first as we receive the best of what He reveals.

It's for His love and His truth, about His peace – the plan of salvation is how we gain and remain in His reach.

With open arms, God has called us to pray both near and far – the true peace of God comes wherever you are.

The more I learn about God, it's where I wanna be – to know better my Father now, prepares me for eternity.

So, I sing to God, I wanna be wherever you are – my joy, my peace, my home is near you beyond the stars.

It's only for His glory that I sing today, to my Father in heaven, I speak to pray.

It's in Jesus, we're worshipping an everlasting King – to honor in glory and the peace that He brings.

Because of His truth, I will always give Him praise, to be in His peace, leaves in my heart joy in so many ways.

On bended knees, I will announce my commitment to the Lord.

God's Spirit infuses the peace for me to remain on this accord.

I can feel the presence of God – I wanna be wherever you are.

It's your peace that I seek from both near and far.

It's the memories that won't let me stop thinking of you.

You're always on stage of the earth for the world to view.

Being thankful for bringing us into the glory of your light – out of darkness to honor you for the blessing of my life.

It's all for your glory that I wanna be wherever you are.

To experience true peace that empowers us all both near and far.

With Jesus; His Spirit is given for us to go the length – doing what's right through His power to give us extra strength.

To feel your Spirit is why I seek your passion – to have both is the best of You that will be everlasting.

I confess true peace is wherever you are; for you, for others I'm reaching both here and far.

I am convinced you are to the world that shining star that brightens the life of those who know who you are – the true peace that covers the world from here to you, wherever you are.

# TRULY GIVING MY LIFE TO GOD

I thank God: He came - my first thought was to solve the basic problems of men; more important is what He did, when He rescued us from sin.

He went back, after proving beyond the shadow of doubt that He was physically alive.

Jesus returned to heaven to be seated by the right hand of His Father's side.

And, when He comes again, it won't be as a baby in a manger; not to be crucified; but to judge the world and examine our lives, to see how and if it's been justified.

With gratitude, I've decided to truly give my life to God.

Doing the right things for body and soul; before it gets shaded by life's highs and lows.

God invites us to be part of His eternal plan – to commit to His idea and make a biblical stand.

There may be people who think they're more spiritual than others – maybe that's true – but would you suffer for your sisters and brothers?

Ask yourself, have I truly given my life to God?

Maybe I'm not where I need to be, for the cause, given His grace – thank God, I'm not where I was.

To all believers, consider this – through baptism we've all taken an oath – to look at the world, filtered through God, we learn the truth about both.

To move and grow in our maturity, we need to move beyond (not away from) God's commands.

Making a decision to truly give your life to God should be your own personal demand.

We must learn to listen to God and proclaim our faith is strong, though we're still weak.

God will blanket us with words of comfort that no other voice will speak.

I refuse to be deprived or denied the inheritance that's offered to me.

I pledge it's my Father's Spirit who I will honestly seek.

Now; if I do, and you won't – will you or should you be in judge?

For that matter – have the right to hold a grudge?

Jesus saves the deepest revelation for those of us who love and obey – we should trust that He'll reward those of us in the most promising way.

Giving a little is still better than nothing at all – one day you're standing firm – reach for the hand of Jesus before you fall.

I've already decided to truly give my life to God.

The concept of dying in Jesus is a supernatural event – because it's beyond human logic is the reason God's angels were sent.

I pray that we all would do all the good that we can, in all the ways that we can, for all the people that we can, for all the reasons that would fit into God's plan.

This is our God – who would oppose the proud to hold a place for the humble.[75]

Expect to succeed and know through Jesus, who will fall and who will stumble.

The need to feed your thirst will be quenched by putting God first, when we truly give our lives to God.

# MOVING FROM SOMETHING TO SOMEONE SPECIAL

As seconds go by – from minutes to hours, from hours to days and from days to weeks – time as we know it, advances to months – the years some eventually reach.

God has designed in this period for something to occur.

Perhaps happiness, or healing, hardship or something else you may prefer.

Whether it's light, or the dark, something large or small – when we look to God, we move from listen, to speak, stand and crawl.

Do you remember when you didn't have?

God turned nothing into something and placed it into your path.

Just when you thought it couldn't be – God did something that only you could see.

The Bible says there is a time for everything, a time to plant and a time to uproot[76] – being something more submissive to commit and follow suit.

There's a time to teardown and a time to build[77] – where there's something of God – words can be your protecting shield.

We all have something in common, if in your heart to believe.

Our God is always where we need Him – in our time of need.

When no one knows; God is the One that will show us the way.

There's something called divine direction and righteousness we hold value in every day.

God is the someone that would transform you – from a person I like into a person I love.

From someone that always looks below, into someone that looks above.

From someone who says I might, into someone who is always doing things right.

From a person that says I believe, into a person who says also I will achieve.

God will transform you into being a vessel – He knows to count on you to make someone feel special.

Are you that someone transformed that God would choose – from something to someone special that God can use?

# MY FRIEND THE HOLY SPIRIT

Who I am is not as important as who I know, my resources are furnished by God – His rewards are what I have to show.

I can walk spiritually and still fall just like you.

But I'm motivated by the spirit of God to do what I do.

And, due to my experiences, I'm being compelled to record my past – hoping that what's collected is beneficial; something that's gonna last.

God thought enough of us to send us a Savior – part of a three-fold trinity that would show us favor.

Preparing our hearts to have a place to dwell – a Holy Spirit that would save us from ourselves.

Remembering those who would cry out with unacceptable words.

Others feel His presence; seeing and saying things they never heard.

For all who believe, we can always count on Him.

With the spirit of angels, God sends His peace with them.

The presence of Jesus promises the Holy Spirit – the depth of my belief is how to come near it.

Embracing God's attributes gives power that's available to us all.

While the quality of my life is enhanced, however I may fall.

Beware of the people who look only for traditional solutions – unlike God's people who pray for the best conclusions.

But be warned, God's Spirit provides extraordinary insight – from your darkest moments into seeing God's miraculous light.

I pray that my friend can be an influence in your life.

All it would take is confessing your sins and believing in Jesus Christ.

The kingdom of God is near – and the Holy Spirit is here, as promised by Jesus, we have nothing to fear.

Whether it's individually or collectively, our prayers will release the Holy Spirit and His power – encourage the confidence of others that God would build every hour.

We are all blessed that Jesus was willing to give what He gave.

The Holy Spirit, a friend who watches over those who have been saved.

The value of friends should become an integral part of life – we should be accountable to God because Jesus paid the price.

# TOUCH SOMEONE AND REACH FOR THE SKY

I wonder: just how much do I matter?

Life at times is sad, though without God it could be even sadder.

Sooooo many not exposed to what God has to offer.

It's rough, but believers with God can make what's hard seem softer.

I pray to the Father – forgive them for they know not what they do;[78] that's the love Jesus has for people like me and you.

Being an opposition, the world would ask: why do we hurt?

We find the answer to such questions as we become the church.

My reply: I touch someone and I reach for the sky.

In order to touch someone, it means I pray for you, in spite of; this is what I do.

So, the others have and I don't, that's no reason to cry; I consider myself blessed when I touch someone and reach for the sky.

To touch someone, I believe we must care – trusting the Lord to not take on more than we can bear.

By God's grace salvation becomes a job; it pays different because it's sanctioned by God.

Everything I am is being consumed by what God has placed in my heart.

As I breathe the love God gave that always measures off the chart.

It's been said that the meek shall inherit the kingdom of God.

Discipling to others about this becomes more than an eight-hour job.

When I reach for the sky, I pray my knees touch the ground.

Finally, I found true purpose in life with God, as I laid it down.

Gradually I am surrendering all of me to the Lord.

Due to the fact He died for me, I've already received life's greatest reward.

From our God a better hope has been revealed with a seal, by which we can draw near with nothing to fear.

Accepting Jesus is how God completes the process with the progress more clear – in pursuit of God, He then pursues you; your temple is the body that has a mind that will feed your spirit which nurtures your soul – a transformation transpires as God reaches His goal.

So, look up, reach out, touch someone about God's plan of saving souls.

A church plants a seed, what happens afterwards is for God to behold.

Each day that we live, as our hearts are beating.

I'm glad it's because of God that we're all still breathing.

So, if you say I am blessed, keep in mind what's been given by you, for you, or by the best.

"God is watching" for you to touch someone.

# MY PASTORS

To my Pastors, I look, hear, and see around the world the best examples that could possibly be displayed.

I've realized that the church, our church needs your emulation of faith every day.

It's tough to walk into a church and find such leaders that are as dedicated to accomplishing any large task against incredible odds, such as Christian Fellowship's men of God.

I am more than impressed; I can't help but thank Jesus for us being so blessed.

I too am convinced that you all are placed in a position of great leadership and may find yourselves overwhelmed by responsibilities, but I do recognize too the natural and your God given gifts that you use to graciously sharpen your abilities.

Pastors, know this: that you all are a light in our lives who has nurtured our hearts on seeking God's good.

So, it is now our prayers that you and your families see and feel the appreciation with love, just like the Bible says we should

God Bless You All!

# EXPECTATIONS

I thank God for a brand-new day – to experience life yet in a different way.

We can all take lessons in glorifying our Creator.

Our blessings would give us now, what might be later.

It wouldn't be unusual for you to expect change when we pray.

When talking to God, we must be careful how and what we say.

To God, some words have different effects than others – what matters is the thoughts behind the words that it covers.

Just like you, God has the right to expect; God has given freedom of choice, to reject or accept.

To every scenario there would be a yes or no, an up or down, an in or out, to believe or not – God has expectations of you going and knowing when to stop.

To go on believing in His Son, Jesus Christ, who gave up His life for the world as a sacrifice.

Because of this, God has the right to expect of you, obedience and loyalty – He who paid the price with His life to be treated as royalty.

God in His wisdom has a purpose for us in His plan.

Satan's plan is to disrupt – the "power of God" is more than he can stand.

Our God created our bodies that come with a soul – given us choices – what to feed our spirit in order to reach our goals.

God has expectations; you would not be conformed to the pattern of this world any longer.[79]

Expecting you to trust, being influenced with His words, with the power to make you stronger.

How would we know what God expects is different from what we intend?

Behavioral change; get to know God – He'll move and remove you from your sin.

If you are focused on the world and all it has to offer, then you've missed God's intentions, therefore your thinking has to be altered.

So, we would choose to allow God; using our bodies for that which has already been paid.

God expects us to accept His salvation - to be forgiven for the mistakes we've already made.

Being the servant that God expects, we should learn to accept; all that belongs to God He protects, God is faithful to those He would elect – that wears the crowns that only He would select, for your good deeds, that's what God expects.

So, we should expect the very best from the Creator.

He's always watching for you to impress, with your godly behavior – always having our best interest at heart, He gave us the Bible – as we grow, we then trust that His words are reliable.

What we can expect from God, now that His Son has made this sacrifice.

We can expect just God; that's worth praising at any price.

# THAT'S THE LOVE OF GOD

Did you know?

We've all inherited the image of God.

One likeness is His identity revealed in His love.

Influences of purity, as expressed in the resemblance of a dove.

It's in each day-by-day God demonstrates the ways He truly cares, the expressions of love are in His words which make us more aware.

Still, some dishonor Him, when prayers replaced with wishes – internally their polished egos dissolved because they're too ambitious.

God is always around: even our jobs – as His Spirit polishes the love of our acts – that don't line up with His facts.

Some may deprive their selves of His love – what a loss – to appreciate Jesus' manger, view it in the shadow of the cross.

And, lean not on your own understanding but acknowledge the Father to never be abandoned.[80]

His grace: like water descends to the lowest part.

He knows you, your thoughts, and especially your heart.

With God, surely goodness and His love will follow me[81] – His Spirit lives inside for the whole world to see.

It's always that time to remember the way it was – if today is any better, then that's the love of God.

Who can turn a curse into a blessing, just for you?

Get to know God, because all that is good is true.

Grow to love the Lord and walk in His ways – as He untangles our lives, we're compelled to give Him praise.

The reality is, if God's not there with you, it's you alone counting on the odds.

With biblical influence, others may witness and know; that's the love of God.

I love it when Jesus declared: I did not come to bring peace to the earth;[82] peace will be with those who love others, but know that God comes first.

It's the love of God when you think about all the sacrifices made – giving purpose to our lives, it's in Jesus' death – that our sins were paid.

In God's love, we can trust in His words to guide – giving us the confidence that He will always provide.

Most churches are grateful to Him to lead us – as we give praise in the name of Jesus – it's the love that only God can give – so you make the choice, let God's love dictate how you live.

# MY DESTINATION

We all have to start our lives somewhere - sinning; until one day we start seeing God everywhere.

Man didn't create man, so to pattern after man – I need God to understand.

Being born into the unknown, it's only through Jesus, I can say I've grown.

No matter how mature you wanna be – our flesh will deny what God can offer us to see.

In the world today, fighting good against evil, how do I find my way?

Knowing Jesus; I'm slow to speak, quick to listen,[83]I've escaped a collision today.

I've experienced worse times than others, seeking Jesus usually gets me further.

I am making progress, moving at a steady pace.

God's providence is guiding me, showing me His grace.

I am sure to go the distance, using God's tools will build my resistance.

My trust is the assurance, added to the faith; covers my belief – my confidence keeps growing, doing things through He that strengthens me.

Which led me to ask: where are you going?

What's my destination?

I'm learning to live in God; He decides my final restoration.

I know when I accepted Jesus my life became heaven bound.

And those who reject will be no more; they are nowhere to be found.

Once you've learned the truth about God and His plan – direction of the world is what? - when we place our life in God's hand.

The map to God is my final destination, discipling to others for a new restoration.

In his journey, Paul said 'though I am free and belong to no man, I make myself a slave' to everyone living in God's land.[84]

Jesus left a path for us to follow with the expectation that one day, with His guidance, we reach our destination.

Everyone is living everywhere trying to keep up with time and space – have you ever stopped to understand how time and eternity are interfaced?

God's Holy Spirit helps me to move with less hesitation, as God in heaven becomes my final destination.

# FAITH, HOPE, LOVE

We all have the mind of a dictionary; where we store those things, which we can call the blessings that it brings.

What we learn may keep us firm, with the impact of an experience, the functioning of our spirit defining deliverance.

Whether into or from whatever and whenever you allow self to be influenced – it adds to your confidence that also builds up your endurance.

Being exposed to the world's resources becomes risky to know what or who to trust.

I'd like to expose everyone to my everything, who answers to the name called Jesus.

If you know Him, then you know God and my friend the Holy Spirit.

The universe's largest corporation: producing faith, hope, love for us to grow near it.

We must all choose a standard of life to live by – with choices; from Jesus and for us from the Most High.

What matters to me is that the world notice and see – that God's word can transform as He reveals more to me.

For some; leaves us willing to grow in other areas of life – at the same time being sustained in the knowledge of Jesus Christ.

And so, I watch to gain in faith and believe – praying with the hope and love I receive.

I'm exposed to this love that the world thinks is dead.

For God has an abundance of truth with love to spread.

In God's sovereignty intentionally there is an anointing that's meant for me; I trust God to give a perspective that only I can see.

So, I watch to gain in faith and believe, praying with the hope and love I receive.

I'm sure there is a before and after I'm exposed to God's truth.

That which is added to your character – that describes the real you.

Without a doubt, I see with faith, hope and love tainted with God from the inside out.

Our Creator and author of the Bible, showing with love what that's all about.

It would be the fruit of the Spirit and His spontaneous work in us – to genuinely help to adopt a lifestyle of the God we trust.

It's about recognizing and then knowing the peace that only God can give.

If man would just slow down and listen – God's attributes can show us how to live.

We all can be exposed to heavy burdens that sometimes penetrate the heart.

It's always something of God that helps us finish what we start.

So, I watch to gain in faith and believe – praying with the hope and love I receive.

At some point the goodness that you are or will constantly produce your growing spirit of faith, exposing your deep gentleness, while sustaining your most desirable traits.

This is delicately inserted as God's objective, 'minus the sin' – it can be assured of leaving space for God to be invited in.

So, we watch to gain in faith and believe – praying with the hope and love we receive.

Only God's word can transform our faith with the hope and love if we believe.

# LIVING IN GOD'S PLAN

Many may be convinced of their ability to live, and do live; without the Creator.

Even though you've contributed nothing to life now, and nothing to offer life later.

All of life's experiences are due to God's grace, and yet you're still here.

And, I can think of God in anything before everything becomes severe.

Believers make better choices when believers choose Jesus Christ.

Because tribulations are unfortunately a part of everyone's life.

I must ask, can you predict the outcome of every human's ultimate goal?

With ideas like Jesus; with the redemptive means of saving all of our souls.

God the Father has offered His Spirit to show us how we are to live.

Once we've accepted His Spirit, we understand better what and how we are to give.

Think about what it would take to persuade you of living in God's plan.

I suggest taking it out of the world, and put it in God's hand.

The Word of God should be our guide to life's decisions, while being watchful of barriers that may lead to our life's divisions.

It would be smart for us to commit to biblical living, in spite of cultural reality.

What matters is our spiritual growth that's above all principalities.

While growing in the knowledge of God; gives us direction.

Reading consistently God's Word is how we keep our connection.

And, though the will of God is within our reach – what matters is how we teach what we preach.

The world should understand that God prioritizes our life.

Obedience in the will, added to the plan, was the calling of Jesus Christ.

To know God is to know He cares more about your character and remaining the dominate factor.

Following, by God's design, is not allowing emotions to be the dominate reactor.

I'm addressing the world and in time the individuals too.

God wants you to be on time as He shows you what to do.

It's in our best interest to accept God for who He is.

Therefore, believe that God's plan is for you fitting into His.

Let's take our lives out of the world, and put it back in God's hand.

So one day, you can honestly say, I'm now living in God's plan.

I'm living here with the hope of getting there; I walk with Jesus in my heart because I'm going somewhere.

It's evident that my destination is God, who I'm determined to reach.

With the gifts the Bible has given me the authority to teach.

I'm now living in God's plan.

# GOD'S DESIGN

In the whole wide world, what's less likely that mankind should receive the credit?

Let's think about the trees and the paper we write on, and the words we tend to edit.

In the Bible, our beginning came when God created the heavens and the earth.[85]

After the fall of Adam and Eve, the order of blame pointed to Adam first.

Ordinarily, men who see with just their eyes, may be victims of depriving their minds.

In the body of Christ, to share in our many parts would be God's design.

The challenge to succeed is given to all of mankind – your attitude about God will determine whether you see or remain blind.

There are some, with open arms; choose God's spirit to be poured in – it's the choices made; that opens doors or closes them; due to our sin.

As the world is rationalizing, compromising, complicating and intoxicating our minds.

Believers of Christ should have had enough; it's time to deepen the implication of God's design.

Where there are two or more gathered in His name – God's presence is felt through Jesus in unity as the same.

Believers should not limit themselves to just the four walls.

Make yourselves available wherever you are to answer God's call.

It's your time, talent, treasures that God is asking you to give.

We're supposed to be new creatures; transparency is how we live.

All this occurs as God grants time and space – it's not wrong to; so, I expect God's grace.

I have a deeper dwelling though I am a sinner; we need to make room for His Spirit to enter.

As we witness to others, let it be known I'm a reborn sinner.

The expectation of Christians is how to be the church.

So the world would understand the importance of putting God first.

Brushing and polishing up the exterior you, will soon show and tell – changed behavior proves that the transformation is more than words to sell.

To live with just expectation of the flesh is not a good sign – but to rid as much of the world's sin is God's design.

Talking to others, be careful what you say, and the way you serve.

The world is so emotional, relationships we'd like to preserve.

If you believe in something you can't see, it just means that you're not blind.

We must continue talking to others and pray because we believe this is God's design.

# WE ARE THE CHURCH

Think about who you are; now imagine who you could be – more or less than others may see.

What defines you?

Is that the same as saying your name?

For God with many, who gets all glory and fame.

Nothing mankind has achieved can compare to our God's power.

Living in this world where morals and values change by the hour.

Believing that it was God who made us who we are.

Since the beginning, explain how man has made it this far.

It's God who gives strength to the weary and He increases the power of the weak.[86]

In return, God would like to know it is He that we would seek.

The world over time has experienced much pain and hurt.

So, God created this institution that He calls the church.

A designated place that was sometimes shielded with four corners and a wall.

Later to become temples in a temple to worship and answer God's call.

The expectation of the Father is not always clear – but our pursuit of His Spirit puts us in His sphere.

Going to church, joining others to be a body of believers, sanctioned by God, set aside from the average achievers.

As we huddle in assembly, God influences the Spirit to edify the soul.

He's preparing His saints to make His cause our highest goal.

Because we live in a lost world – Jesus; we need not search, His Spirit dwells in the believers, and we are the church.

It's for His cause we lift up holy hands, praying and working together we learn about God's plan.

Our efforts will grow and grow into an enormous amount.

We learn about not counting your days, but making your days count.

God needs us all to function in order to have an effect.

As God becomes the master of your heart, then that's what we'll reflect.

The strength we acquire should not be dictated by the way we feel – who we'll becoming will understand better – to perform what God has to reveal.

The work God would have us do - emotions should be indicators, not dictators.

So, discipline your hearts to always be alert – honor our God with dignity, because we are the church!

God's intent is for us to influence the world and all of life.

Get involved – be the church that draws others to Christ.

Because I am the church; you are the church; we are the church, believers truly believe in putting God first.

Together we can have an impact when families have lost their way.

Let's be the church that carries our cross for God every day.

God has given us dominion over the earth – and wherever we go, we are the church!

# HERE I AM, I HAVE COME TO DO YOUR WILL

In the beginning, and to every beginning is where something begins – creating an origin is where the Creator created His creation without any sin.

Life was His idea, for His reason, to serve His purpose.

He included us in His grace; without it we are worthless.

God's deepest desire is that the world would admit they're related.

All He would love is to fellowship with the people He created.

Our God is a giver, for us to receive, we must learn to be still.

God, here I am; I have come to do you will.[87]

To know God starts with a first step – buying into His pay-it-forward concept.

God has created a formula, in which faith is the main ingredient – to obtain the attributes to live in His providence, it's moved by your obedience.

Your belief, can be seeded by your experience, influencing your history.

The closer to God we are, the nearer we're drawn to victory.

Let's live by faith – in order to witness God's word being fulfilled.

Just say, 'here I am God – I have come to do your will.'

We must grow in faith; and as we're growing in the process, we're becoming more spiritually inclined – with hope for success.

My God has established His plan – that requires a human face.

Don't abuse or misuse freedom of choice; God awaits to give you, His grace.

Not all God's children are just – some are willing to make a biblical correction.

We must accept the blood of the crucifixion in order to reap the resurrection.

No doubt, God is mysterious, but in time will expose Himself to bring out your deepest skill.

And, by your will – you are here to do only God's will.

Because God knows you, you should know too where giving God our devotion has little to do with your emotions.

Living in this world, with tribulation, having God would be essential.

Knowing Him would bring out the best of your potential.

God has set aside the old ways to establish the new from within.

Pleasing Him would be to approach with faith, not only by abstaining from sin.

How long must the Lord tolerate your defiance – before you individuals agree in compliance, to become in total reliance?

Our God is more than worthy, for some His love has been defined – let's invite His Spirit to write this in our hearts and mind.

Mankind is destined to die once, that is precise;[88] let's choose to live for Christ, for our God Himself is waiting to change your life.

Do you desire your life to be fulfilled?

God awaits – surrender to Him and let's do God's will.

I am blessed in my work produced by faith, laboring prompted by love, with endurance inspired by grace.

It is my prayer for Your word to be fulfilled – here I am Lord, I have come to do your will.

# A COVENANT JUST FOR YOU

What is in heaven is to be emulated here on earth.

In other words, on earth as it is in heaven would be the expectation of, He who created it all.[89]

We can position ourselves with God to be ready at any time to answer His call.

He has given us a manual and tools to be prepared.

How we receive God's presence would reveal just how much we care.

God would prove to be the founder who possesses all truth.

His words speak to your troubles, sending angels to your rescue.

God's design with all promises has proven to be words of fact.

There is no part of life that His truth can't impact.

"Ya see" – there's God's word and then there's justice, and there's justice in His word.

Our pursuit should be to attach ourselves to the Word of God in order to be purged.

His covenant was made just for you; you would first believe, to be drawn closer to His truth.

It was God who said "I now establish my covenant with you and with every living creature that is with you too."[90]

All of humanity is made in God's image, creatively this is your self-worth.

Hearing, learning, and following God justifies our existence as here on earth.

God will punish those who continue to sin and act out against Him.

Then reward thousands who follow the commandments, as He displays His love for them.

In the old covenant God ordained priests to stand between Him and all the others.

Under the new covenant all believers become priests, confessing and praying for one another.[91]

This is your position of influence for the good of God's truth – once again a covenant was made just for people like me and you.

We can all testify that the old covenant was a shadow of the new – God gave His only Son; He gave His blood and His life for me and you.

It was also God who created the covenant of marriage between husband and wife – a bond with spiritual purpose which together He prepares you for life.

Jesus once said; "this is my blood of the covenant which is poured out for many."[92]

Later He said the seal of an agreement that will bring to us plenty.

A covenant made just for you – that will bring you closer to God's truth.

Throughout God's word – for those who haven't heard.

Available is the cleansing and renewing of our hearts, which is for the salvation that sets us apart.

God promises to breathe new spiritual life into His people's heart, causing the brokenness of each servant to have a brand-new start.

His covenant; which was made just for you, bringing you ultimately closer to God's truth.

# TASTE THE LIVING WORD

Are you convinced that the gift of life began with God creating man?

Our freedom of choice, determined by what, where and how we live in this land.

The Creator has provided food that some choose to waste.

God too has a recipe for life, often displayed in His grace.

Satan will lead us to feel as free as a bird.

But God has conditions for life, once you taste the living word.

No doubt we were all born into sin – systematically given the Holy Spirit to change deep within.

It's no myth what can be achieved through the sacrificial lamb.

Between the world and God, I personally am building a dam.

The world needs to know: with Jesus what's the big deal?

As He lay me down to sleep, His Spirit helps to consider what's real.

I suppose it to be good, a sheep under the shepherd's herd.

Being led to eternity by the lamb, when we taste the living word.

Through His Son is our start to a new foundation.

This concept is attached to Jesus, free of condemnation.

Can you envision man's functioning successfully while here on earth?

It was once the original plan before the revelation of Jesus' birth.

Some believe there is eternity; and there's time and space.

Jesus was sent to lead us home, to the eternal place.

I pray that the church stands on its convictions, in spite of what's been heard.

As the church teaches God's truth, from the Bible, we taste the living word.

# LIKE JESUS

I'm lying here staring into a clear blue sky – as I ponder why.

My purpose: pleading for destiny is what I cry.

Innocent as anyone could be, realizing true purpose isn't up to me.

My standard of living isn't just for my good; as I grow, I've learned I couldn't change a thing if I could.

I'm dealing with these emotions inside of me, and nothing has to do with the way I feel.

I want change; but fortunately, my fate has already been sealed.

"Like Jesus" I expect some to follow, but none like me – because I have some visions much different than they can see.

I'm realizing the older I become, the more I'm consumed.

The world at times will pause; through Jesus, I'm built to resume.

Like Jesus, from the first day, to the world I'm meant to be more than a brother.

I've been given a mission, and to accept the burden of others.

For now, I've acknowledged that I am unique.

If you have the humility to admit you're flawed – you and I should speak.

"Like Jesus," know this: the popularity isn't my goal – gradually I'm learning my purpose includes saving souls.

My focus is to have some impact on other's attitudes, to enrich the population.

I like to think my influence could be the means to your salvation.

"Like Jesus," I'm grateful to care about everything that has been given to me.

Suggesting that you make the choices that would set your heart free.

Everyday I'm reading and learning, and praying, and then I read to learn how to pray, adding the love with prayers; while praying your soul hears what I have to say.

"Like Jesus," my desire is to do my Father's will so that I keep growing – to impose the opposition with confidence and walk away knowing.

"Like Jesus," I defend we are subjected to sin with no intent.

Like Jesus, we're born of God's Spirit and saved by His grace.

I'm offering prayers for every man of every race.

"Like Jesus," the word of God teaches me to speak of hope – even when others are trying to provoke.

To walk in salvation, we listen as God the Father speaks, learning as God the Son is baptized, His words will set us free.

It is no mystery, in God we begin to trust.

Learn to accept as God the Holy Spirit feeds us.

"Like Jesus," blessed are the pure in heart for they will see God.[93]

By embracing His love, we're experiencing victory against all the odds.

We go to church to become God's church and we share with others what we've heard.

We can expect spiritual growth as we rely on God's word.

To emulate Jesus, we should wear His kindness from the inside out.

Displaying His kindness with love, that makes you wanna shout.

"Like Jesus," be kind spirited that inspires others.

Praying constantly for all your brothers.

Kindness that penetrates the heart – kind ways that bring people together, instead of tearing us apart

To see a glimpse of what Jesus looks like – is reflecting His character through you.

Being like Jesus is in the actions of what we do – others will see Jesus when Jesus is living in you.

# FILLED AND COMPLETE

I confess, I was once lost; nothing seemed to matter but being my own boss.

Though it did take time for me to find a better way – through the storms of tribulation, God brought me where I am today.

Still, time after time we all face life's defeats – hoping to someday feel rich in heart, while filled and complete.

The world has its own recipe for success in our lives – I'm learning and being guided by God's Holy Spirit to be my eyes.

There are some people who look for points of disappointments, sowing seeds of disregard.

Sometimes it's God's will for His people to resist Satan trying to make things hard.

Because God is who He is, that's enough for me – Jesus paved the way for even the blind to see.

For all who have welcomed Jesus as Lord into their lives, are spiritually filled.

Now to reap God's benefits, we must listen for what He has to reveal.

Believing that God can send us heaven bound, destined for easy street – mysteriously He lives in me; now I'm filled and complete.

Because I now know Him, I make it known – God opened my eyes to care for more than just my own.

I can trust that I am where He wants me to be – with God's word, we can all be filled and complete.

We should all react to good advice my friends, allowing His Spirit to be a deterrent to your sins.

Finally, I am convinced to have a God seeking persistence – I've accepted that He has always been the overseer of life's existence.

Being filled is knowing Christ came to save the lost – committed to the mission with God – I'm not just wearing my cross.

Through prayers I have a chance to be complete – God's word says I'm filled – to know His grace is what I seek.

I refuse to allow circumstances to dictate me – God would pour in us, His truth for the world to see.

I know now that God is all we need to be filled and complete.

# HIS LOVE I NEED

I myself do serve the Lord with fear.

Somehow, I feel obligated to stay near.

Jesus' love for people with His attributes deserves an applause.

Receiving His peace comes with accepting His cause.

Something philosophers would like to know, being uncertain that He's real.

How does He maintain three entities and still be a good ideal?

There is a part of the world that truly knows Him – and there's the other part who think He means nothing to them.

For those who don't know – Jesus sacrificed His life for you, and God is the one who sent Him from heaven just for you.

Within His sovereignty, He makes available His Spirit for all of you.

That's the power of love; from God the Father – the Son and the Holy Spirit, for you.

I confess, I am who I am because of nothing I do.

It's because God loves people like me and you.

Our Father in heaven loves first His Son and placed all in His hands.

Perhaps, we too should practice His love; to fit ourselves into God's plan.

In His plan, He implicates a sacrifice, by His will, that was made.

Attaching our lives to this concept is the way to eternity, while being saved.

So, being aligned with God, as a sacrifice, what should a man give up?

Perhaps our sin – for us, what has already been given was far too much.

While the world seeks fulfillment in the pleasures that they adore.

God expects His children to seek Jesus, and receive so much more.

God's love is something offered and still in great need.

It's not an emotion, but a more characteristic decree.

My desire to know Jesus is knowing I'm receiving the best.

Influencing my spiritual growth, as He's influential to my personal success.

This love that God has, the same love that Jesus shares, something that the Bible shows us how to declare.

Into our tribulation, we sometimes fall, only to find ourselves lost.

Jesus will pick you up, carrying you while you carry your own cross.

Believers know His love is something we need.

Lifting our burdens, Jesus touches our souls to be freed.

Through Jesus is ultimately the way to God's heart.

This becomes supernatural that manifests into a work of art.

We can all pray day and night, not asking for much.

But whatever we pray must be accomplished through Jesus' touch.

Again, I proclaim that Jesus' love is strongly in need.

We must be careful to insert Him into our lives, His decrees.

It was God who created the man that caused condemnation, and then He gave to the world another man to fight temptation.[94]

Encouraging others to seek this power of love that Jesus has, we need to be assured of God's promises to receive all of His love indeed.

# "CHRIST"

When the world was: way back when, and we were all but a thought.

When we and earth were being planned, God's Spirit was the earth's only salt.

So, God created man and gave him a name.

As creatively God was; now names don't mean the same.

What has a name ever done for you?

From what perspective would you like to view?

Our God was once addressed as "I Am" and Moses took that to the promised land.

God would use whoever, however, whenever He chooses man to make a stand.

He would nurture and carry you until His Spirit teaches how to become a man.

If the name doesn't match the man, God may see a need for change; unlike mistaken identity, God has the right to re-arrange.

Through time, sometimes our names can be a factor – in the absence of God's Spirit, anything can be a distracter.

A better focus would be where God can give us an alternative for life.

Through a name that never changes, the name of Jesus Christ.

In every category of life, this name can be the past, present or future.

As prayers are being said, God shifts His focus to the user.

History reveals His legacy; within eternity through time and space.

Being the character is more valuable than names on a face.

The man in Christ grew, as Christ grew into a man.

It's not the man who makes Christ, instead Christ who makes the man.

I believe without God we cannot, and without me, God will not.

God's revelation is somewhat powerless without man to react, because man is God's creation, to move at all is based on that fact.

So, Christ's reaction would be to end with an appeal – He who has ears should use them to hear.[95]

In the words of God; has much to say about Christ.

We should listen to the Creator with His ideals about life.

Every human is born once, but only some will die twice.[96]

What dictates the inevitable is your name in the book of life.[97]

Ya might wanna know: since the beginning of all things, God reshaped His order – by putting Christ as the head of church; we reap the rewarder.

Here's my testimony: If Christ lives in me and He is the church, then the lost souls who look for salvation should include me in their search.

I've accepted the salvation that God has offered to me, as the world has access to the same spiritual liberties.

For the name above all other names is Christ.

Better known as the Messiah, our Lord and Savior, Jesus Christ.

# KILL THE SIN, SAVE THE SOUL

Where there's death, we exist no more.

And, to repent is the door to be restored.

Think about who of this world would you follow?

Allowing the influence of someone with a heart that's hollow.

Why is there a right and a wrong?

With others can you determine when it's best to get along?

We all live with the hope of growing old.

So why do we feed the body and not the soul?

"Imagine" – we collect with our minds and believe in our hearts.

But it's our spirit where spiritual growth starts.

Born into the attitude that grows deep within – acknowledging God would be the method to kill the sin.

My character: being my identity, that's who I am, so I'm told.

I intend to learn God's truth, to eventually save my soul.

It's the fear of change that frightens people of changing their ways – Satan has enslaved their thoughts; leaving hope in the saint that prays.

Let's focus on the process – that God would grant, if man would think 'can-do' instead of 'I can't.'

We need to see ourselves through God's spiritual lens.

There's only one thing that God can't do – it's sin.

Observe the saints who have grown up to be old – not by chance, it's a miracle to behold.

In this life, it is sometimes easier said than done – I trust myself to trust God my battles are already won.

There is with certainty; we must continue to grow in all areas of life – the most definite way of doing so is getting to know Jesus Christ.

To get to know our God; learn about the sin He hates.

For the sake of others, you should be saved before it's too late.

For the seeds that we would sow – God changes the hearts; who looks for spiritual growth.

This is God's process of killing the sin - that saves the soul.

If my falsehood enhances God's truthfulness and so increases His glory, why am I still condemned as a sinner?[98]

It's the intent that influences the heart to repent, so our choices that we choose would make us a winner.

I vow to kill the sin to save my soul.

To re-establish the lifestyle with biblical goals.

I regret that I was born into this world of sin.

But through prayers the Holy Spirit helps to make amends.

God has given us the means to do away with sin.

Transforming souls is to be concerned with what the spirit takes in.[99]

We don't evaluate this flaw with man's measuring stick – with your love for God, His truth is what will convict.

With God I must kill the sin and save my soul.

To honor Him with righteousness, and the integrity that He holds.

I belong to God, all of my body and mind, my spirit and soul.

We must worship our Father with our ways to achieve our spiritual goals.

That's keeping the door open that kills the sin that would save our souls.

# A TIME OF CHRISTMAS
# THAT CHANGED YEARS

As we grow older, we're in sync with the world's traditions every year.

Collecting the old and new – something for our families to see, say and hear.

Some of us may delight in change, while others improve by staying the same.

I wonder, what would be your value in life?

If you haven't been introduced to Jesus Christ.

A time of Christmas comes at the end of every year.

And, we are judged on how we give, not allowing the world to interfere.

Giving is integral in describing the nature of our Creator.

His giving, when gave, is how some would get to see later.

Here's something for even the blind to see in this story – in the real Christmas, the world should be singing to His glory.

In different messages, God announces that Christ has come to offer salvation.

Angels of the Lord were sent to put in motion songs of His revelation.

Portions of the world had long since gone astray; though churches have been ready to worship that first Christmas day.

Godly people should not poison this season of its original intention.

In every act of Christmas, my Lord Jesus Christ should be mentioned.

There are many episodes in the Christmas story which have been displayed.

The celebration of a Savior – from our hearts is what needed to be made.

Christmas changed the year – a time of Christmas that changes every year.

Born a time to remember it's the words of Jesus we need to hear.

A cry from the world's perspective: seeing is believing, but from God's perspective, believing is seeing.

I believe in the Lord – as I should – can you taste and see that the Lord is good?

Because of Jesus, I'm redeemed to worship God for the wonders of His creation.

Jesus influenced my spiritual growth, seeded by our heavenly relation.

It's through Christ – the reality of relationship with the God of Peace – a message of assurance was fulfilled in this birth of Christ to say the least.

Purifying us from sin is what should be properly seen – accepting the blood of Christ – all sinners have now been redeemed.

This is what Merry Christmas means.

You can now expect royalty – worshipping our newborn King.

May the voices of all the angels sing – with the sacrifice of a Savior, we can now be redeemed.

So, with the gift of Jesus our souls have someone to lead us.

Reconciliation between God and humanity is a celebration of the Christmas way.

We too can celebrate all God's creations in every day – singing Merry Christmas to Jesus, who has given us more reasons to pray, while celebrating God's creations with love from day to day.

This lasting gift of Jesus who promises to always stay near, giving us the hope that Jesus will bring us change every year.

And now that you have been made more aware, in the gift of Jesus; will you not share?

# FATHERS

In honor of this day, I was inspired to write this poem, titled *Fathers*.

I believe that sometimes we as fathers are inspired by the Holy Spirit to act on our inspirations.

Making good decisions, with God in mind, always come with great admirations.

There are many characteristics of fathers spread out over this earth God created.

Among the good, bad, saints and various nemesis, none are better described than the Father named in Genesis.

Our Father dear – to whom His love commits us here.

In honor of the All Mighty, it's because I fear.

Every day we pray for You to be at our side – to breed life; into your light, to guard, to rule and guide.

Fathers encourage the young men to be self-controlled,[100] while our Father in heaven continues to bless our soul.

In your teachings show integrity, the seriousness and soundness of speech; it's because fathers who know the Father, prayers will reach.

As some may know like us, God has a Son who was born and died.

An attitude not to give up, young men should know that Jesus is alive.

Be encouraged to accept Jesus Christ, speak with maturity for the young man's life.

Honestly, to be an excellent father you must learn from the Father to be a good father.

Understanding Jesus is in spirit with knowing fatherhood, God is watching; fathers do what you know fathers should.

Congratulations to all the fathers, both young and new.

"Please" nurture the misfortune because God has His eyes on you.

# ONE FATHER AT A TIME

Our God in heaven would be the best teacher on fatherhood - Putting our lives in His hands means being ready to do whatever is good

Knowing your heavenly Father enables us to relate to our earthly fathers.

There was once upon a time we were all but a thought - and then came tribulations that weren't even our fault.

When man was born, God had a design – to build up man one Father at a time.

I'm convinced that there's more to fathers than seeds of conception - being weak minded or strong has no value that would make you the exception

Our heavenly Father has created us in His image -man and cultures of all kinds.

Descended from the beginning of Adam, to Abraham and Moses – one father at a time.

It's perhaps overdue to put a new face on what fathers are supposed to look like.

Count the times you're on your knees asking God how to do things right.

God's word teaches that we should recognize Christ for His saving work – after all He became for our sake – the end of the world's starving search.

It's in the name of Jesus;

Fathers we are justified – and God blesses those fathers who have been sanctified - I know that through the Holy Spirit we are edified - It's then for our salvation; with God we are unified – and so shall we be thankful – for He's worthy to be glorified.

Now for the mature; make sure that your example is motivating younger believers, to live in a way that honors God and produces young achievers

It's men among saints who are looking for us to show some kind of sign - something godly that would encourage them – one father at a time

I may not be the man that I want to be - I may not be the man that I should be - but at least I'm not the man I once was - that man didn't believe nor had the faith to believe in God.

We can't always build a future for our youth - but we can build our youth for the future, one man at a time - We need more fathers to teach young fathers how to be better fathers by honoring our Heavenly Father

One Father at a Time

# AN ANGEL IN DISGUISE

Blessed is the saint that works for the Lord.

Those of us who choose His words over guns and swords.

Weapons of peace and acts of love are just as real – put in the right heart to carry out what God has willed.

Our Father is a master at using prophets, deacons, pastors, and angels too.

I believe He empowers the weak and the work that they do.

So, let us pray when needed – that we may have our own angel in disguise – working in our favor to teach and enhance our Christian lives.

"Which bring to mind" – Pastor Stan Archie – one of many men that God has gifted and given his own vision – to lead His people at CFBC from the confusion of life's spiritual decisions.

Can't imagine his journey started with ease – what some believe is far from what God sees.

The gifts this pastor possesses are unlike any other.

God knew it first had to be nurtured by his gifted mother – as the Holy Spirit took control of this man's life – God then put in his path a saint named "Evelyn," the perfect wife.

And just like us, they needed motivation too – so God delivered little ones to add to his spiritual crew.

As he grows; they grow too – a delightful element for God to view.

Added to this spiritual growth is the church – handiwork of God's transformation.

Compliments to all the other pastors who help build our church foundation.

# A HEART'S DESIRE

We trust in the One who allows us to dream.

Guided by His light, our lives may be redeemed.

While God appoints and anoints those in our path.

In your heart – understand what God says we can have.

It's our heart's desire – that God plans to prosper you, not to harm you.[101]

While sending pastors to lead you.

Good leadership is a blessing, especially when we're in the right place to receive.

There are some who are deprived, those who have not in their hearts to believe.

Christians at CFBC have been blessed to have such leaders – Gadson leading his team of worshippers, encouraging new believers.

The passion that he and his family display is transparent, showing how they care.

Though their voices are a sweet melody – the Gadsons' touch hearts everywhere.

I've learned our pastor is addicted to worshipping the Lord – it's in his blood – always preaching and teaching how to come to this accord.

Pastor Gadson is being led by God to lead others to do His will – pouring his voice out so that the hearts of God's people may be fulfilled.

He is a heart's desire.

# SEEK TO KNOW GOD

I've learned that too much of anything is not as good for you as other things.

An example is knowing too little of God is not healthy for spirit or soul.

And, eating too much – the right kinds of foods are bad, yet we still grow.

Our bodies are the temple of the Holy Spirit. [102]

As we honor God, we expect to be drawn near Him.

Having a source should be the means to everyone's resource.

Learning to know God is a convincing recourse.

I seek God to know God; to some nothing else matters.

To a world who doesn't know God, I pray their world never shatters.

Ya see, because I seek Him, He's seeking me – this means I'm under His protection.

Acquiring God's attributes is a way to live with assurance of His correction.

Acceptance is the key to making the initial transition into God's family.

The objective becomes moving toward God – to grow away from the world's calamity.

In this world today, there are those who know God and those who know of God.

True believers understand; wherever God's concerned, you're either in or out.

Salvation is God's introduction to Jesus; whose Spirit lets us know what He's about.

As we seek God, His Spirit pours a measure of Himself into us.

Getting to know God is possible through His Son Jesus.

Because God is the Creator and ultimately the world's only Master.

God should be the inspiration that keeps us safe from the world's disaster.

The Bible says to seek first God's kingdom to know and do what's right[103] – too much of ourselves in anything influences a different way to fight.

To withstand any fight, should be our fight with faith.

God being our source of strength who's available for everyone's sake.

My prayers are for every man's soul to be led by God's Spirit alone – seeking to know God would be the better choice of any evidence ever shown.

I believe in God and I trust in God for who He is – mankind needs to be reminded, God is in control and this world is His.

All the more reason that we as a human race should always seek to know God to experience His grace.

# SEEING THE UNSEEN

Let's close our eyes and take a walk with God.

I remember my first steps; to be transformed, "It's Jesus that I must accept."

God's word has given me a Spirit to enhance; because of redemption, I now have a second chance.

There's an order we should follow in this redemptive process, committing to God's plan is the hope of having spiritual success.

We can come to understand our purpose and what it means – as we grow, the Lord will give out portions to see the unseen.

How much of the world shares in the Holy Spirit – that you try to reflect?

Can you honestly say your character has a big influence with that godly affect?

There's a world out there who are blind to what God has revealed – not only saints have access to God's truth about what is real.

We need more; who choose to do God's bidding by joining the team, you too will be given the keys to the Kingdom of seeing the unseen.

And there is no need to fear – "God is here" and He's always there.

Living under His cloud means that His protection is with us everywhere.

We live in a world where angelic beings do exist – only by God's commands do the angels give humans assist.

God does have a biblical agenda to pour into my life.

That can start with acceptance of His son Jesus Christ.

In a vision I can see God when I pray – I can see God when I sing; I see God when the sun shines and the happiness that it brings.

Because I accept; I've been redeemed.

Even with my eyes closed; I can now see the unseen.

# SEEING BEYOND THE GOAL

We're looking – but can we see?

We feel – so should we touch?

When we listen, do we really hear?

God speaks to our hearts – salvation is what keeps us near

To believe in God requires little faith - life or death for our souls is what's at stake.

Do you believe to have faith, or have faith to believe?

Seeing is believing - that's man's design.

But God's reasoning – we can't live by sight and faith at the same time.[104]

Look around and watch the lives without God unfold – take note of your faith – learn to see beyond the goal.

There's faith we gain and there's faith we lose – examine the feelings that cause you to be overruled.

God's word is the fuel to our faith

We should strive to be disciples for other's sake

Staying in God's word protects and shields our soul

And having faith is seeing beyond the goal.

The thing God hates is His people continuing in sin

I believe this can short circuit our faith deep within.

Satan's tactic is to influence you to doubt God, never to please us

But staying in God's word is what anchors us to Jesus.

So when little faith slips and takes its toll – just stay focused and learn to see beyond the goal

Struggling faith requires more than just belief

Enroll in God's training and pray to be released

His word is designed to grow us in faith

It's a level of assurance that blesses us in every way

With no faith we look at obstacles as it couldn't be and should be, not as it was

What if we used that effort to read our Bible and keep our focus on God?

Then we can move from mature faith to great faith; from great faith to perfect faith – the position of being confident of a protected soul, unlimited in prosperity that we can now see beyond the goal!

# MY DREAMS

Could my dreams be my desires?

Or, could my desires be also my dreams?

Sub-consciously whatever our thoughts, neither may be what it seems.

I confess my dreams start with God and end with mankind – choosing to conform to God's word, transformed by the renewing of my mind.

What are dreams?

Maybe divine guidance that comes only to prepare hearts – "I believe" God always finds a way: this would be a good place to start.

The beauty about this is that in spite of what you've heard, sometimes it's best to remain quiet, even when we'd like to have the last word.

Could our dreams be a vision of something we'd like to see?

I would invite your sub-conscious to come dream with me.

As some may hurt for change, we all have something we need – my dream is that we live without sin, eventually come to God and be freed.

From me; for my brothers-n-sisters, as in the body of Christ.

Live for each other as our spirit feeds the soul to live a better life.

This is my dream, that I pray for you and you for me – so at the end of the day – we've all grown wiser about eternity.

We must prioritize our lives by the values outlined in God's word.

With acts of righteousness, we move forward to our voices being heard.

Only by God's grace; we have a mind that understands, eyes to see, ears to hear; God makes us all possible, and He's the only one I fear.

Don't expect God; but respect God, and accept God, as we reflect God, for all His favor.

Put God first and then you can expect to eat the fruits of your labor.

It's the sin that divides us; without it, who knows – it's eating culture after culture, too bad we've all been exposed.

There's no hope of measuring up to God outside of my dream – salvation draws us closer to God – influencing the world to be redeemed.

It's about knowing what's best and doing what's right.

We belong to one God, don't let this be about black or white.

In my dream, in pursuit of one perfection, I do see a limit; according to God's standards, it's more than academic.

In my dream God is teaching us to have voices of influence, to have no thirst for sin, and an attitude of endurance.

This is my dream, that it may become yours, and that we all share the same dream of being with the Lord.

# MY DREAMS OF ETERNITY

Our God, the eternal God is very real, and the love that He has offered is branded with an eternal seal.

If you think you have a God given gift, thanks be to God who showed you the way.

From health to your wealth, God offers us an abundance of everything to add each day.

To fear the Lord is the beginning of a new wisdom, deserving all praise.[105]

I suggest: submit to the cross and much will be added in many different ways.

Our God is the true God, the living God and the eternal King – His plans for the world include you accepting His truth and the joy that it brings.

God's existence in everything has a purpose that reveals His vision.

We should appeal to His presence to apply Him to our life's decisions.

It is a must for us to understand our purpose in God's plan – so search for your purpose that fits your life in God's hand.

God has standards for us to live while living in our search – His will be done – if we're learning better how to live as the church.

God Himself is the standard of life which we are to live – as we trust in God, He touches our hearts and shows us how we are to give.

We should all be in search of God's perspective – we first should address it, then we engage the collective.

It's sometimes a glimpse of eternity, the way God would display His love.

"Jesus" – a pattern by which we emulate the purity of a dove.

Thanks be to God, we all have that freedom of choice, others will know as we exercise our freedom of voice.

Looking from the outside in, how do we get this eternal life?

It starts by knowing God Himself, through His Son Jesus Christ.

This life on earth can be an introduction to eternity.

If your pattern of life is adjusted from internally.

If we can receive this new life with faith – the effectiveness is evident when our life begins to elevate.

The experience from an eternal perspective can be subjective – but seeing it real only with God's objective.

If having a goal would be your passion led by God's desires to match, then His design for your life would be all you need to attach.

Jesus said, whoever hears my words and believes in Him who sent me, has eternal life.[106]

We have the choice to be the disciples of the world, empowered by Jesus Christ.

With Jesus, pray to share in His vision – to please God and be driven with His mission.

Yes! I have a dream to be led to eternity – edifying my spirit, while being transformed internally.

In this journey to eternity, some will earn their crowns for God, from God, to give back to God.

The expectation would be how His servants choose to live – fulfilling the dreams of eternity is what He has to give.

This is my dream, what about yours?

# THAT'S WHAT MOTHERS DO

To all God's people: let's take a moment to say thank you heavenly Father – so much evidence of the love – need we ask?

Why does He bother?

Passed down His Son from one righteous to another – the first born of God and a first-time mother.

The world would ask: just who are you?

Mary: God chose me to do what mother's do.

A precious child was born in a manger – with a special mother God kept from danger.

There became a time, this mother would be protested – it was in the name of Jesus, already she was protected.

Though Jesus is firstborn, He was not above the law – rejected by some, the rising of many is what His mother saw.

Our God provides when the time is right – which includes giving mothers that special insight.

God allows mothers, and then He lifts up mothers, He blesses mothers to be something a bit more than special too.

Maybe you can understand why mothers do what mothers do.

Why not invite God into your heart?

If you haven't, now is a good time to start.

So, the world is filled with injustice and abuse – godly mothers are protected from the world's tainted misuse.

Know that God's favor doesn't always bring instant success – but through our prayers builds confidence that our mothers are truly blessed.

It was the blessing of Mary that allowed her to be a mother of inspiration.

So, in God we trust to give us a heart of all admiration.

God has continued to use the mothers to carry out His will – we too can allow the Holy Spirit to empower us with God given skill.

The absence of some men tears down what a good mother builds up – but God sends out to all mothers an angel with His special touch.

God: He designed families – that requires fathers too – but a household isn't godly without a mother to do what mothers do.

# CONNECTED TO A MOTHER

I am but one more saint who prays to God – seeking His spirit to advance my steps – and hoping that prayer is as hard as it gets.

We sometimes expect more from some than others.

So, it's a blessing if you're connected to a mother.

God provides most with a comfort to their needs, especially His children, those who confess, proclaim, and believe.

What is a mother if God didn't provide?

Who's being a comforter if she didn't decide?

God created and designed everything about earth – everything about school, home and the church.

I thank God for His creations, for you, me and for others.

I would also pray for those who are not connected to their mothers.

Man has no right to proclaim that she was put here for me.

Even though she gave the forbidden fruit, he ate, which came from the tree.

We could search for the why's and the who mothers are put here for – I think it's by design; God has intentions of so much more.

Consider this: when man becomes partnered with a woman, and whatever he lacks – he can rely on a mother to always have his back.

Not all women can be the mother that could pass God's test – today you can work on the balance of saying more and doing less.

When mother's interests are put aside to focus on others – it's a biblical experience if we're also influencing one another.

Where God and mothers are respected, long life can be expected.

You will be blessed – when you and your mother are connected.

If our connection is any real, this is how Christians should act: you can expect God and His mercy to refurbish anything we lack.

The trinity decided: man would not be alone, so, then came others.

God designed the wife, from that came mothers.

In God's family His concept has planted an ideal, that all families emulate His goodness – as scripture has revealed.

Connected to your mother can bring peace with all others, it's the influence of God that influences all mothers.

With or without God, the world can be destructive – when mothers are connected to God, life can be productive.

God has asked that we care for our brother, and feel privileged to be connected to your mother.

# LOVE OF SISTERS

Here's a toast given to one, requested by them all, led by each other, to see that no one falls.

Bonded by their love which can't be replaced – their relationship is protected by God's common grace.

They're all very special; their attitude is no one's better than the other, easy to see because they share the same mother.

This love of sisters is rooted by the oldest – she does stand strong, with a unique boldness.

Celebrating their youngest day of birth, this family has been gifted since their feet touched the earth.

Yes, this love of sisters, to say the least, has been put to the test, but I'm so glad now I can thank God – they've all been blessed.

One for all they're all for each other – they're driven by the love that pushes them further.

They all believe that there is a God, and He's our creator.

Beliefs are hard to convince others; to believe that God is greater.

The sisters have a love for each other that is impenetrable – believing that anything driven by God makes them this short of being invincible.

The love of these sisters is spreading their love everywhere they go.

Thank God they're bonded, and, their love is what they have to show.

# HONORING ONE THAT'S HONORABLE

It's the request of our heavenly Father to love others more than ourself – though honoring Him with love over anyone else.

Believing in God means to inherit His ways – emulating our Savior can literally change your days.

We are given His gifts to do His deeds – planting His words in our mouths, in our minds, til we finally believe.

God spares us only this one life – to get better at our choices – then to do it right.

Beatrice Johnson is one of those saints who truly loves the Lord.

Something you can see in her actions – by God's strength she's learned to push it forward.

God loves her because of who she is – and she is a lover of God not because of just what He can give.

In her walk with Christ are included many ingredients.

She learned long ago how to pray for His grace – and the value of obedience.

To many she's known as Grandma Bee – to know her heart – that only God can see.

I pray of all the gifted population – she's among those who has the recipe for salvation.

Like Bee; let's stay in touch with God and "Pray for your brothers" – so we aren't carried away by the wrong influence of others.

If you've accepted God's invitation; then He lives in you and me.

Knowing how she has; for as long as she has done the things she has done – God lives also in Grandma Bee.

What an honor, to honor someone like her who understands the glory of life – which is to love, not to be loved, to give – not to get – to serve, not to be served.

To honor one who honors others more than one's self – while honoring the Most High over everyone else.

Beatrice Johnson's life is praiseworthy of honoring.

God bless you Grandma Bee!!

# OUR VALENTINE

Gentlemen: If you would be so kind, take the hand of the one you call your valentine. Remembering that very first romantic twine – you decided to yourself; God, I'm gonna make her mine.

Now it could have been the face, the hair or a smile to make her look so fine, but thank God it grew into a relationship that makes her your valentine.

By God's standard this should be a forever sign, but history shows mistakes that make us glad we never crossed the line. Note that Jesus is the Master with relationship. Whenever we fall down – He finds a way to pour in love – n – compassion when no one's around.

God created matrimony in the beginning of time – isn't that an emulation of what man calls 'my valentine?' Regardless of what it is called, the two are to become one til the end of time. That's if you honor God by mastering His design. It's the relationship with my mate that I can say is mine.

We belong to God and He knows she's more than just my valentine.

# A TESTIMONY

<u>How I've Grown in My Salvation</u>

Remembering that salvation is deliverance from the power of sin, deliverance from danger or difficulties. Also, deliverance of being rescued or redeemed from… or recovery of an unwholesome lifestyle. Another perspective is being saved; something that can start at any time. As we grow to know God's character, we also grow in our salvation. Wherever you are in life, God will tailor fit salvation on you. And, even if you undress God's Spirit from you, God will restore your salvation once it has been given (Psalm 51:12). We will learn how to tell the stories as God leads us to be the story. God and His promises will be offered to all who believe and desire to be in God's family by establishing a personal relationship with God. And, this could only be accomplished by believing in God and coming to terms with the fact that we all need God's salvation; and we can't save ourselves.

Eternity is what God is offering to the world, and it starts with an acceptance of His salvation. Eternity means forever and forever only exists in heaven and we go to heaven after accepting salvation. The acceptance of salvation conditioned with the belief in God's Son Jesus Christ can we be reconciled into this relationship with God. Only with this approach do we open this relationship.

Time after time God would reveal to mankind a little of His character, His love, His compassion, His mercy, and His promises through the hearts and minds of His creations. As He instructed

Moses, (Exodus 6:6–7), "Therefore, say to the Israelites: I am the Lord, and I will bring you out from under the yoke of the Egyptians. I will free you from being slaves to them and I will redeem you with an outstretched arm and with mighty acts of judgment." God will always fulfill His promises, but it is always a mystery how and when He performs these different tasks because His timescale looks different from our time and space. But His way is the only way. In many aspects of life, Jesus tells us what we need to know, and obedience is an important role in our fulfillment.

In our journey of life, Jesus points the way to heaven and eternity (Matthew 7:13–14). The gate that leads to eternal life. This does not mean that it is difficult to become a Christian. But only one way to live eternally with God. That one way is believing in Jesus Christ is the only way to heaven, because He alone died for our sins and made us right before God. We all should thank God for giving us a way. It is our choice to enter through the narrow gate. For wide is the gate and broad is the road that leads to destruction. But small is the gate and narrow the road that leads to life, and only a few find it.

"Jesus is the way." God sent Jesus to earth to save us; to do so "by the Father's will," became compelling for Jesus to teach us the way. In a life lesson format, Jesus teaches about salt and light (Matthew 5:13–16). Jesus said we are to be the salt of the earth. By accepting Jesus, we become a seasoning flavor of His Spirit being prepared to be the light of the world. Like a city on a hill cannot be hidden, in the same way, we are to let our light shine before men and women, that they may see your good deeds and praise your heavenly Father. If Christians make no efforts to affect the world around them, they are of little value to God. God doesn't want us to blend in and look like the world, but instead we should be more of an influence on the world than the world has on us.

Be not ashamed of the gospel, (Romans 1:16–17), because it is the power of God – for the salvation of everyone who believes: first for the Jew, then for the gentile. For in the gospel a righteousness from

God is revealed; a righteousness that is by faith from first to last, just as it is written: The righteous will live by faith.

There was a time early in Jesus' ministry, He went up on a mountainside and called to Him those He wanted, and they came to Him (Mark 3: 13–19). He appointed twelve, designating them apostles that they might be with Him and He might send them out to preach and to have authority to drive out demons (Matthew 28:16–20). In God's kingdom He always makes provisions. God gave Je

sus authority over heaven and earth. On the basis of that authority, Jesus told His disciples to make more disciples as they preached, baptizing and teaching them. With this same authority, Jesus still commands us to tell others the good news and make them disciples for the kingdom. If you are a Christian, you owe much to others who have taught you and modeled for you what you needed to know about the gospel and Christian living (Hebrews 13:7–9). We should continue following the good examples. Though human leaders have much to offer, we must keep our eyes on Christ, our ultimate leader.

Moving forward we must realize some Christians still cling to Old Testament ways of living, such as not eating certain foods. In that time this was important to salvation. But now those laws are useless for conquering a person's evil thoughts and desires. The law could influence conduct, but they could not change the heart. Lasting changes in conduct begin when the Holy Spirit lives in you. And, the Holy Spirit lives in the people who believe and accept Jesus as the Lord and Savior of their lives; another promise fulfilled. It is better for our hearts to be strengthened by grace, not by our attempts to keep God's laws or ceremonial diets.

So I say, live by the Spirit, and you will not gratify the desires of the sinful nature (Galatians 5:16–25). If your desires are to have those selected qualities of Jesus Christ, then you know that the Holy Spirit is leading you. Being led by the Holy Spirit involves the desires to hear, the readiness to obey God's word, and the sensitivity to discern between your feeling of emotion and His prompting. The Fruit of the Spirit should be our overwhelming influence if we want to live the life that God has to offer. Fruit of the Spirit must be experienced in order to impact, and impact the world in your present environment. We need to better understand those qualities of the Fruit of the Spirit from God's perspective.

For example: our definition and expression of love is not the same as by God's standards. Here we offer some kingdom living suggestions. God's spiritual fruit consists of (1) love – beyond human experience, deeper than just an emotion; it's the highest form of love. (2) Joy – a deep rooted contentment in God's sovereignty. (3) Peace – wholeness, assurance of God's justice and agreement with His sovereignty. To have a relational experience with these principles, we should intentionally apply them by practicing them as we come to understand them.

To learn and grow in these areas of life, we need to understand better the method in which we grow, which is: our experience, our history, and our influence. And, as we grow, here's how we exercise them biblically: love people, worship God and use things. For example, we shouldn't use people selfishly with no regard or love things with an attachment that only benefits you and self-gratification. And, worshipping anything outside of giving glory to our heavenly Father. With the potential of receiving favor from God, we shouldn't practice any of these outside of this order. That's the way God can better use you or us to serve in contributing to His kingdom agenda.

As we grow, we will eventually start to think like Jesus and mimic His ways to the point of having a mind of Christ as it states in 1 Corinthians 2:15–16. No one can comprehend God, but to learn His character through the guidance of the Holy Spirit, believers have insight into some of God's plans, thoughts, and actions – they, in fact, have the "mind of Christ." With consistency, moving closer to aligning our minds with Christ. To have a positive impact in your environment wherever you might be, we should have a biblical impact, with a biblical intent. Understanding better our roles, our identity and our assignments from God's perspective. We should understand those attributes of God, have a different meaning than that of the way the world thinks.

Paul gave evidence of the lack of love in the utilization of spiritual gifts. Although people have different gifts, love is available to everyone. Love is patient, love is kind. It does not envy, it does not boast, it is not proud. It is not rude, it is not self-seeking (1 Corinthians 13:1–7). It is not easily angered; it keeps no record of wrongs. Love does not delight in evil, but rejoices with the truth. It always protects, always perseveres. Now if your love doesn't look like all that, then you and I have work to do. It's our choice.

As God is my witness, this is also my prayer for you, that your love may abound more in knowledge and depth of insight (Philippians 1:9–11). Often the best way to influence someone is to pray for him or her. Like Paul's prayer for the Philippians was that they would be unified in love. He encouraged their love to result in greater knowledge of Christ and deeper insight. And, that their love would not be based on feelings alone, but on what Christ had done for them. As we grow in Christ's love, sour hearts and minds must grow together. With this overview, how does your salvation measure up?

Remember those earlier days after you had received the light, when you stood your ground in a great contest in the face of suffering (Hebrews 10:32)? We don't usually think of suffering as good for us, but it can build our character and our patience. Even for someone whose blind, our perception won't always be reality. But for someone who sees with more than just their eyes or feels with more than just emotions, your perception can be your most reliable reality.

As God has given, we to must learn how God wants us to give. It's easier to do what's right when we gain recognition and praise. To be sure our motives don't waver into selfishness, we should strive to do our deeds quietly or in secret (Matthew 6:3–4), with no thought of reward. In this area of life, Jesus might suggest: Matthew 6:6 regarding prayers, and Matthew 6:18 in generosity and fasting. In those acts of life, we should not be self-centered, but God centered. While reaching for God's hand, ask yourself: "Would I still have done this if no one knows that I did it?"

Luke 1:30–31 talks about that submission that leads to favor from God. Though God's favor doesn't always automatically bring instant success, being submissive to God is an act done without thinking of concerns about consequences, especially when it comes to fitting our lives into God's plan. In Mary's case it was part of God's plan to bring about our salvation. Don't allow circumstances to dim your hope as you wait patiently for God.

Wearing your best attitude, remember, finding salvation requires more concentrated effort than most are willing to put forth and give. Obviously, we cannot save ourselves – not to mention those who don't believe that they need to be saved. We can't work our way into God's favor. It's not about taking the next step, but how you get to the next step. The efforts we make in getting there and the motives behind the effort that we make is what matters to God. We should keep in mind; God's methods are to develop us from the inside out. The efforts we must put together to enter through the narrow door is earnestly desiring to know Jesus and diligently striving to follow Him, no matter the cost (Luke 13:24–25).

We would do well to see Him as the 'Eternal One' who came in the flesh. But who, then was He before He came? To see that; we need to see the Apostle Paul's unique telling of the incarnation in Philippians 2. In Paul's teachings he's suggesting a reflection of what our efforts should look like. He starts an eternity ago in our heavenly Father's presence. He gave us four characteristics of Jesus as God so that we have a clearer view of Jesus before coming to earth. (1) He's the God who serves: Jesus was humble and willing to give up His rights in order to obey God and serve people, developing a servant's attitude. (2) He's the God who departed and arrived (Philippians 2:6) – Jesus was and is who? Although He existed in the form of God, who being in very nature God, note the incarnation was in this act, the pre-existent Son of God voluntarily assuming a human body and human nature without ceasing to be God. "How is that for supernatural?" (3) He's also the God who sacrifices: Philippians 2:6 – who did not consider equality with God something to be grasped – He did not give up His deity to become human, but instead set aside the right to His glory, to become submissive to the Father's will, to be the example of what God expects of mankind. He was and is Jesus, the sacrificial lamb for mankind's sin. In order to re-establish reconciliation with mankind and God, that which Adam disrupted in the beginning of earth. (4) And then He's the God who empties Himself – emptying His humanity into a servant with the servant's attitude and with the likeness of man. In some, the challenge for man mimicking or adopting this lifestyle is man allowing too much of humanity to overrule their perspective and attitudes, not allowing God's standards to become more of their standards. And they believe it's their right. But from God's perspective it may be the misuse of freedom of choice. It can start with you, and then you and Jesus, and then with you and the Holy Spirit, and ultimately reconciling you with our heavenly Father – God. I think it is the best choice for our souls.

From the beginning of mankind on earth, as time progressed through the Old Testament of the Bible. God gave to mankind laws to live by called the Ten Commandments. And, no one that belongs to mankind is exempt or excluded. The very first of mankind on earth demonstrated to God that it is virtually impossible for man to live by His Ten Commandments without trusting God. But God established another plan to His plan for man to live by. A plan that gives mankind the freedom of choice. As mankind approached the New Testament, God's plan started to unfold. And the most important piece to this puzzle began to reveal to life, that we can be saved by accepting the man named Jesus Christ. Ultimately, in total submission to Jesus Christ is the only way any of us can be reconciled to God, to live with God in heaven forever it is required of each person on earth to accept Jesus Christ as your Lord and Savior of your life.

Although to that extent, God knows that desire will never be fulfilled. Some will perish not accepting the truth, not believing that Jesus died for our sins. For that you will die once and when Jesus Christ returns again, you who do not accept will suffer a second death. So, it is in our best interest to believe and accept that Jesus died in our place for the sins that we committed, so that we can live in eternity with God forever. This is salvation growing in me, as I grow in my salvation. I would invite any and all to come grow with me.

# ENCOURAGING WORDS

The Purpose and Benefits From the Old Testament Into the New Testament From God's Perspective

Romans 5:20–21

The law was added so that the trespass might increase. But where sin increased grace increased all the more. So that, just as sin reigned in death, so also grace might reign through righteousness to bring eternal life through Jesus Christ our Lord. As a sinner separated from God, you see His law from below. And, as a sinner, you desire to seek God, curious to know who He is, His character, what comforts of life might He offer to you as an individual or collectively as a family.

So, you make these attempts of what you think is good or right way of doing deeds that you feel God should approve. Only to climb upward and fall yet again and again because your way isn't getting you closer to God than when you first felt the need to pursue this journey. These attempts amount to different hurdles of life which we struggle every day, trying to do the right things, trying to keep the law and live it. The sovereign Lord that we serve knows of your struggles and knew of your difficulties.

Romans 8:3–4

For what the law was powerless to do in that it was weakened by the sinful nature, God did by sending His own Son in the likeness of sinful man to be a sin offering. And so, He condemned sin in sinful man in order that the righteous requirements of the law might be fully met in us, who do not live according to the sinful nature but according to the Spirit. So, from the Old to the New Testament, God's ideal was long before set in motion, since the beginning of mankind, God realized the weaknesses and vulnerabilities of the human nature. So, He offers a redemptive idea, one where you don't have to rely on your individual will or strength.

Romans 13:8–10

Let no debt remain outstanding except the continuing debt to love one another, for he who loves his fellowman has fulfilled the law. The commandments to not commit adultery, not murder, not steal, not covet and whatever other commandment there may be are summed up in this one rule: love your neighbor as yourself. Love does no harm to its neighbor. Therefore, love is the fulfillment of the law. "Ya see," God loves His creation that much. God's idea is salvation from the inside out which He offers to the world, and it is or should be life-changing. In God's system of doing for His creation, He reveals to us in portions the way to redemption. God created the body with a spirit that carries our souls, which is really who we are; a body that collect with the spirit that feeds our souls and that determines your personality, integrity, your characteristics, behavior, your attitudes, your honesty, your patience, your gentleness, your sensitivity. The way we forgive and all those qualities that are internal of the body.

God's idea is to transform us from the inside out by offering salvation with the freedom of choice, in order to transform His creations to be children of God – to live with Him in heaven where our real home is for eternity, that means forever. All these godly attributes are the fruit of the spirit which can be nurtured with God's Spirit by accepting His Son Jesus Christ. It is the only way mankind can be redeemed and reconciled to God.

John 3:16 says that God so loved the world that He gave His one and only Son – that whosoever believes in Him will never; he said 'never' perish, but will live forever. Not in your present body, "He's even giving us" a new body. For those who live for God now will live with

God in heaven forever. To receive this blessing accept the offering of Jesus Christ as your Lord and Savior of your life. Surrender yourself to Jesus and He will prepare you for heaven; to live with the Father.

It's a long journey to walk these steps, but God supplies us with the map, so we don't get lost, but even if we do lose our way, we'll never be alone. God will be looking down on us, Jesus will be living with us, and the Holy Spirit will be living in us. Helping us to have a secure journey, where thousands are reduced to hundreds and before you know it, He's right by your side. Absent from the body, present with the Lord. AMEN!

# INDEX OF POEMS
## BY CATEGORY

## Spiritual Growth

a. Salvation
b. One Father at A Time
c. Taste the Living Word
d. I'm Living on the Street of Faith
e. My Destination
f. Living in God's Plan
g. Seeing Beyond the Goal
h. A Time of Christmas that Changed Years
i. Purpose
j. Where is God?
k. Faith, Hope, Love
l. Seeing the Unseen
m. In the Image of God

## Devotion

a. My Valentine
b. Moving From Something to Someone Special
c. Fathers
d. That's What Mothers Do
e. Gifts and the Gifted
f. Touch Someone and Reach For the Sky
g. Where is God?
h. Always Wearing Your Best
i. Faith, Hope, Love
j. The Words "Let There Be Pastors"
k. Connected to A Mother
l. Filled and Complete
m. That's the Love of God

## Admiration

a. Honoring One That's Honorable
b. A Heart's Desire
c. An Angel in Disguise
d. My Pastors
e. Connected to A Mother
f. Death to My Father

## Behavior & Service

a. Here I am, I have Come to Do Your Will
b. Can You Imagine?
c. Like Jesus
d. Jesus is the Way
e. The Words: "Let There Be Pastors"

## Influences

a. The Titles We Choose to Wear
b. The True Light
c. My Dreams of Eternity
d. My Dreams
e. Expectations

## Prayer Life

a. A Believer's War Room
b. His Love I Need
c. God is the Perfect Ingredient
d. The True Light
e. Kill the Sin, Save the Soul

1 Genesis 1–2

2 Genesis 1:1

3 Genesis 1:24–25

4 Genesis 1:20

5 Genesis 1:31 – 2:3

6 2 Corinthians 4:16–17

7 2 Corinthians 4:18

8 2 Corinthians 5:8–9

9 John 14:27

10 Philippians 4:6–7

11 Psalm 119

12 James 1:22

13 Romans 12:2

14 1 Timothy 5:17–18

15 ibid

16 Matthew 5:45

17 Matthew 6:19–21

18 1 Corinthians 3:13

19 1 Corinthians 15:33

20 Romans 10:14–15

21 Acts 9:1–19

22 John 14:6

23 Ibid

24 Hebrews 4:16

25 Genesis 1:1

26 Matthew 16:24

27 John 14:6

28 Galatians 3:29

29 John 15:1

30 Romans 12:2

31 John 15:26

32 John 17:4

33 Romans 6:23

34 John 13:12–17

35 Ibid

36 Genesis 1:26

37 Hebrews 11:1

38 Psalms 23:1

39 Psalms 23:2

40 Psalms 23:3

41 Psalms 23:4

42 Psalms 23:5

43 Ibid

44 Psalm 23:6

45 Deuteronomy 29:29

46 Genesis 1:1; Job 38:4

47 Matthew 16:24

48 Revelation 20:12–15

49 John 14:6

50 Romans 8:37–39

51 1 John 1:9

52 Acts 1:8

53 Romans 12:2

54 Genesis 2:15

55 2 Corinthians 12:9

56 2 Peter 1:2–4

57 Genesis 3:1

58 Hebrews 11:1

59 John 3:3–8

60 Genesis 1:22,28

61 Genesis 1:26

62 Genesis 2:18

63 Isaiah 64:8

64 Matthew 13:16

65 John 4:10:2

66 Romans 12

67 Hebrews 4:12

68 John 8:36

69 James 4:6

70 1 John 2:1

71 Luke 15:10

72 Hebrews 1:14

73 Luke 6:38

74 1 Corinthians 2:9

75 James 4:6

76 Ecclesiastes 3:2

77 Ecclesiastes 3:3

78 Luke 23:34

79 Romans 12:2

80 Proverbs 3:5

81 Psalm 23:6

82 Matthew 10:34

83 James 1:19

84 1 Corinthians 9:19

85 Genesis 1:1

86 Isaiah 40:29

87 Isaiah 6:8

88 Hebrews 9:27–28

89 Matthew 6:10

90 Genesis 9:9–12

91 1 Peter 2:5

92 Matthew 26:28

93 Matthew 5:8

94 1 Corinthians 15:45–49

95 Matthew 11:15, 13:9

96 Revelation 20:6, 14

97 Revelation 20:15

98 Romans 3:7

99 Philippians 4:8

100 Titus 2:6

101 Jeremiah 29:11

102 1 Corinthians 6:19

103 Matthew 6:33

104 Habakkuk 2:4

105 Proverbs 1:7

106 John 5:24

Printed in the United States
by Baker & Taylor Publisher Services